LEADING BETWEEN
TWO WORLDS

LEADING
BETWEEN
TWO WORLDS

*Lessons from the First
Mexican-Born Treasurer
of the United States*

Rosario Marín

ATRIA BOOKS

NEW YORK   LONDON   TORONTO   SYDNEY

ATRIA BOOKS

1230 Avenue of the Americas
New York, NY 10020

First Atria Books trade paperback edition June 2007

1 3 5 7 9 10 8 6 4 2

ATRIA BOOKS is a trademark of Simon & Schuster, Inc.

Manufactured in the United States of America

For information about special discounts for bulk purchases,
please contact Simon & Schuster Special Sales at
1-800-456-6798 or business@simonandschuster.com.

Library of Congress Cataloging-in-Publication Data
    Marín, Rosario.
        Leading between two worlds : lessions from the first
Mexican-born treasurer of the United States / by Rosario Marín.
            p.   cm.
            1. Marín, Rosario. 2. California—Officials and
    employees—Biography. 3. Politicians—California—
    Biography. 4. United States. Dept. of the
    Treasury—Biography. 5. Hispanic American women—
    California—Biography. 6. Hispanic Americans—
    California—Biography. I. Title.
    F866.4.M37A3 2007
    324.2092—dc22   2007002717

ISBN-13: 978-0-7432-8645-9
ISBN-10:   0-7432-8645-6

Contents

Preface   ix

Part One: **LA FAMILIA**

1. Articulating Darkness   3
2. The Voyage   12
3. Life B.E. and A.E.   41
4. Spiraling Downward   58
5. A Family Is Born   71
6. Living with Purpose   87

Part Two: **A POLITICAL LIFE**

7. Bridging Two Worlds   97
8. Acting Locally   114
9. The Judas Kiss   124
10. Treasuring Opportunities   143
11. The Chance of a Lifetime   177
12. Mexican Homecoming   185

Part Three: **WORDS TO LIVE BY**

13. Blazing a Trail   193
14. The Successful Seven   206

Acknowledgments   273

Preface

Some people are certain they have a book boiling inside them ready to spill out onto the page. I was not one of those people. The way I saw it, the main ingredients of my life were more or less like anybody else's. And yet, over the years I continued to hear many versions of the same question: "Have you ever thought of writing down your life story?" I was flattered by the suggestion but never envisioned myself as an author. I had played many roles in my life: daughter, mother, wife, banker, advocate, and politician. All of these I could handle, but being an *author*? My first language isn't even English. Besides, where would I find the time to even begin inscribing my life onto the page? Perhaps one day, I thought, but there was just too much going on right now.

Then, one day it happened. Johanna Castillo, an editor, called and asked me the same question I had been asked for years. Here was a young ambitious Latina asking me to share my life with readers. Like me, she wasn't born in this country and, like me, she was constantly striving for success. If my story could reach other Latinas like her then it would certainly be worth the effort. I had to be honest with myself; there most likely would never be an ideal time to write a book. As I have often said, the best time is now because that is all we have.

I didn't know how an "author" began writing a book, but I thought pecking at my computer's keyboard might be a good place to start. At first I was hesitant to be as honest as I knew was necessary, but before long there was no stopping me. It turns out that everyone was right, I did have a book boiling inside of me and it was spilling out onto my keyboard; my fingers frantically tapped in an attempt to keep up with my thoughts. I never did find that large chunk of time I imagined needing to write. Instead, I was able to take advantage of stolen minutes while waiting for connecting flights and meetings to begin, and in the early mornings before going off to work. Soon the pages began to accumulate and I was faced with a sizable pile of paper that—through the efforts of many individuals—evolved into the bound book you hold in your hands. To all those people throughout the years who urged me to write down the story of my life, here it is. It was a process that often felt like I was describing a dream.

I suspect this is because I *was* capturing a dream that could only have sprouted on American soil. The American Dream that is fueled by a pursuit of happiness is the fundamental story of this country, and my life is a grateful reflection of its reality. It's a story worth retelling because it serves as an example for others—especially Hispanic immigrants who are now members of the fastest growing minority in this nation. When I arrived in this country over thirty years ago, I could never have imagined that I'd one day sign my name onto its national currency as the forty-first treasurer of the United States. I have often said that becoming the treasurer during President George W. Bush's first administration is more telling of the possibilities of this country than of my abilities. Had my parents decided to immigrate to any other nation, it is doubtful that I would've become its treasurer. In 1972, as a fourteen-year-old girl sandwiched between her mother and sister on a bus heading to the U.S., all I could think about were the family and friends I was leaving behind in Mexico. Little did I know the adventure that lay just around the bend.

I firmly believe that the United States is still a great land of opportunities. It pains me when I hear the lack of appreciation that some of our citizens—many of whom were born here—display for the freedoms we are granted. As a nation, we do have our problems, but the fundamental values this country was founded on still hold it strongly together. When I hear this ingratitude, I only wish I could buy these people plane tickets to witness what it's like to live in other countries and not just vacation in them. I've had the opportunity to visit many great nations and I'd never consider leaving the United States. What other country has citizens who speak over one hundred languages and come from every imaginable corner of the earth? Although we may speak many languages, the one that binds us together is expressed as hope, opportunity, and optimism. I know that for every person who has achieved the American Dream, there are several who may not. There are myriad reasons this is the case, but I believe America, at the very least, provides the opportunities to create a life worth living and worth capturing in a book.

The story you are about to read takes place in several countries and has characters that I love and hate. It is filled with anecdotes, lessons learned, and both painful and joyous memories. In short, it's filled with the material that is life. For every page written there were five left unwritten. Few lives could fit within the confines of a book. I had to be judicious in choosing which events to share with you; if I erred in any of my decisions it was on the side of conveying the moments that best revealed who I am. My story begins with sharing what was once my most closely guarded secret. Although this book is far from a confessional, I was honest—whether telling you about my fears before making love for the first time or how I dealt with political betrayal. You'll be right alongside me as an event divides my life in two, I struggle through depression, I create my family, I participate for years in local politics, and I become the U.S. treasurer. Life isn't neat and tidy. With me, the political and personal often overlap and, due to my convictions, are often one and the same. My hope is that you will find the main character in the pages that follow interesting enough to stick with her as she relives the good times and the bad.

What drove me during the entire writing of the book was not a need to share my life story or bare my soul, but an ulterior motive that fully reveals itself in the final section of the book. It is my attempt to reach a broader audience than would ever be possible from speaking engagements or personal interactions. Yes, it's advice from me to you. Although I would never claim to have all the answers, I do think I have something to offer—especially to young Latinas and immigrants who too often don't dare to dream the American Dream. I always tell them that if I could do it, so can you. What I've been able to achieve in my life is not due to luck, charm, beauty, or anything else that is often attributed to quick success. I did, however, have values that were expressed in the seven actions that I share with you; they have made my life one that I'm proud to share. No matter who you are or where you find yourself at this exact moment, know that you can do it, too. *¡Si se puede!*

PART ONE

La Familia

1. Articulating Darkness

Lean in close, I need to share a secret with you. To fully understand it, I'll need to take you back to 1963, to the root of the darkness: a place where one of the most painful experiences in my life once festered. I was a bubbling five-year-old in Mexico City and, like many children, I was afraid of the dark. Nightfall unfurled itself like a vast canvas on which I painted my troubling thoughts. I'd nudge awake my younger sister Margarita, already soundly sleeping next to me, and ask her to accompany me to the bathroom. I'd pray and pray for the fears to go away, but they remained my constant companions. I didn't fear some unidentifiable bogeyman lurking in the shadows; no, he was a lot more real than that. While I struggled to fall asleep, the source of my fears was most likely roaming the streets. Night after night, I'd consume the darkness of my secret like a vial of poison, waking up with an acrid taste still stinging my tongue. The morning sunlight would play on my face—signaling the start of another school day—and the sweet smell of my mother's cooking would waft through our small house. The spell would be suspended until the following night when the vicious cycle began again like a deeply scratched record that only I could hear.

My grandmother was eighty-seven years old when she passed away in 1996; she would never know the secret that swelled inside me, her beloved *nieta*. At the time, I believed the revelation would have been too heavy for her to bear—crushing not only her, but also my entire family. It was a cross that, unfortunately, didn't become lighter with the years. I dragged it around so that no one else would have to. Now I know that some crosses were never meant to be carried alone, especially not through darkness. It would be eighteen years before I would gather enough courage to share the secret for the first time, tearing through the dark canvas of the night to set down my cross. It was only then that the healing would begin.

Casting Off the Cross

His beautiful mustache twitched to life as articulate words flowed from his mouth. To my nineteen-year-old heart, this was not only love at first sight, but I was certain I'd marry this man. Alex didn't know it at the time, but he had captured my heart during the closing ceremony of Encuentros (Encounters), a religious retreat.

Flash forward four years: it's a week before our wedding, a time when I should've been a carefree twenty-three-year-old about to marry her first love. The darkness that had plagued me since I was a child began to come to life in my dreams. I'd wake up in the middle of the night drenched in sweat, feeling as though someone was suffocating me with a pillow. These weren't prewedding jitters, I couldn't be surer of anything. My body was telling me it could no longer carry on with the weight that had grown on me like a tumor. If I was going to live the rest of my life with Alex, I'd have to find the words to share my darkest secret. He was the first person I'd tell and no amount of rehearsing could've helped. I was plagued with doubts about how he would handle the news. I worried about how I'd change in his eyes. I knew I could lose him.

It ended up coming out in one long monologue, punctuated by guttural sobs. I took a deep breath and . . .

"I was five years old. I had already learned my letters and numbers, so my mother was able to get me into the first grade by telling the school that my birth certificate had been lost. It seemed to do the trick. At our school, first graders were released an hour earlier than other students. My mother didn't want me to cross the busy main boulevard to reach our house, so I waited for her at my grandmother's place near the school. One day my grandmother's brother—a slovenly, perpetually unshaved man in his late forties—came out of the cramped room that connected to the house and told me that my grandmother wouldn't be home for some time. I didn't know much about him other than he'd always leave early in the morning and return late at night. Anyway, he told me to come and sit on his lap, but I said no, that I'd just wait for my mother. He insisted, grabbing me by the shoulder. Then, then . . ."

Alex held me close, sensing how difficult this was for me. He waited calmly for me to continue.

"Then, he started to touch me down there and all I could do was shout no, no. I cried and cried. It didn't make a difference to him. Sometimes at night, I could still feel his breath on my ear, whispering that this was our secret. I was confused, but each time I resisted more. He then tried to lure me with chocolates or a few cents. I told him that I didn't want them. It didn't matter; his hands would creep down again. One time I went to the bathroom and through a small crack in the window, I could see his feet pacing, waiting. I began to fabricate any excuse possible for my mother to pick me up at school. Then I started to stay at my aunt's house that was even closer to the school. I felt like this was somehow my fault. I was deeply ashamed."

I looked up from my knotted hands into Alex's eyes and prepared myself for the worst. Although it was probably only a few seconds of silence, it felt like an eternity. My mind raced with the concerns that had weighed on me since our engagement: What if I wasn't a virgin and he didn't want to marry me? What if he'd look down on me? What if he was angry that I hadn't told him sooner? What if he did marry me out of pity, then divorce me? Oh my God!

"You have the right to leave me, I might not be a virgin," I said, breaking the silence, while attempting to steady my breathing. Tears continued to drench my cheeks.

With gentleness and caring true to his nature, Alex wiped my warm tears away, reassuring me that none of this had been my fault. He was sorry that I had lived with this burden for so long. He held me close, telling me that he loved me for who I was; something horrible that had happened to me when I was a mere child could not change that.

I realized then that I would forever be in love with this gentle soul. I felt an indescribable, almost physical lightness after sharing my secret for the first time. It was one of the most painful, but ultimately cathartic experiences of my life. It had taken years to gather the inner strength to shed light on what I had believed would remain a repressed and inarticulate darkness until the day I died.

A week later, on September 19, 1981, we were married in Saint Matthias Catholic Church (our local church) in Huntington Park, California. It was a beautiful ceremony that I will forever remember. I never felt more certain about anything in my life as I did on that day. Nothing else seemed to matter. I imagined creating a family with Alex. Although he was only twenty-four at the time, I knew he'd be a wonderful father. The future it turns out would be full of surprises—some of them wonderful and others devastating. At that moment, however, surrounded by the most important people in my life and linked arm-in-arm with this wonderful man, I couldn't imagine being any happier.

That night and for many nights that followed, we would not consummate our marriage. Everything was smooth sailing up until a certain point when I'd get too tense and couldn't go on. No amount of coaxing seemed to work. The fact that I had the blessings of my family, the church, and the state didn't make a difference: I could not share this wonderful experience with my husband. One month passed, then another, and another. Three months had gone by and we were both frustrated and upset. My husband tenderly suggested that I see a doctor and I promptly made an appointment. The doctor said that, physically, there was absolutely nothing wrong. His expert advice: a couple of glasses of wine to relax me. Not surprisingly, the wine didn't have the intended effect. I continued to freeze. The doctor suggested I see a therapist. I couldn't have agreed more.

It was soon to be New Year's Eve—the first one Alex and I would celebrate as a married couple—and I wanted that night to be "the" night. When we returned home after bringing in 1982, I began to sob uncontrollably. I told Alex how horrible it made me feel that I couldn't show him how much I loved him.

"Rosario, if all I wanted from you was sex, I would not have married you," he said, pushing a strand of hair behind my ear. "I love you for who you are."

Those words permanently engraved themselves into my heart; it felt as though something deep inside me shifted. Alex had validated me with pure, simple, and loving words. My fears dissolved as though a spell had been broken. That night, I became Alex's wife. It turned out that despite my worries, I gave my virginity to Alex.

Afterward, I turned off the bedroom light. I felt a sense of peace as I wrapped the once-frightening darkness around me like a warm blanket. I slept more soundly than I had in years.

Now Is the Time

So now, at forty-eight, why have I chosen to publicly reveal such a private part of my life? Maybe because the more we talk about such atrocities, the less they will happen. Maybe it's so at night, when I wonder how many children and now-adult victims are also awake at this moment, they will have a bit more courage to tell someone their own dark secrets. Maybe it's a reminder to others that no matter what traumatizing event they've had to endure, time and support can help them move beyond it.

I have accepted that certain scars will always mark me and I've vowed that I'll no longer go out of my way to hide them. That would be playing the true victim. Healing takes time and love from the people in your life you can trust. Until the moment I shared with Alex what happened, I had been living a double life. Telling just one person made all the difference. I do have one major regret: keeping it hidden for so long. To think that I carried such a weight on my shoulders for nineteen years now seems unfathomable. Once I conquered my fear of revealing my secret, it became increasingly cathartic to share it with people. Each time I share my experience with someone, I feel a bit lighter.

This will be the first time that most of my family, friends, and colleagues will learn about what happened to me as a child. People whom I have known my entire life will be reading about it at the same time as people I will never meet. Many will be shocked, having never suspected a thing; this is a testament to how hard I've tried my entire life to appear worry-free and happy, especially when I was a child.

Everyone has always seen me as such a strong person that the last thing I have ever wanted to do was let them down, or be seen as a victim, even if that is exactly what I was. I never wanted people to pity me. Later, I entered politics and did not want to risk politicizing something so painful. I marched on as long as I could, head held high, trying hard to never look back and to rationalize my continued silence.

My reasons for silence varied. Life seemed difficult enough for my family and finding out that their daughter had been molested was the last thing they needed. I was afraid that something bad would happen to my family, or some sort of scandal would erupt. I wished death on the man who molested me many times—and then one day he did die. The pain of what he did to me lived on, but I had been taught never to speak ill of the dead. Then I convinced myself that it would just go away. It happened so long ago that it would somehow fade into the recesses of memory. At the very least, I predicted, the pain would diminish.

Now I know that such traumatizing events should not be forgotten. I also know that it isn't just one thing that helps with the healing. It started with my believing that what happened to me was nothing to be ashamed or embarrassed about. There is a world of difference between saying something isn't your fault and that you shouldn't be ashamed and truly feeling it and moving on. It continued with my sharing my experience as a lesson for others. After I initially talked about what happened with Alex, it was another four years before I could bring myself to tell my mother what her uncle did to me. The silence that surrounds these social taboos, especially in the Latino community, is deafening and rests on the collective shoulders of thousands of children and adults. I have met many people who have shared their experiences with me and, unfortunately, their stories are variations on the same theme. In almost all cases, it's a family member or someone close to the family who abuses a child's trust. There is no way around it: when something this devastating happens so early on in life, it fundamentally alters the way a child will perceive the world. Often the marks are even evident well into adulthood.

Not too long ago I met a voice coach who, upon hearing my voice, gently suggested I had been molested. I was shocked. How could he know? It became evident that the scars that wounded my spirit were recognizable to those trained to see or hear them. All hope is obviously not lost. Millions, like me, are proof that early adversity—in any form—can be overcome successfully, but the burden should not be carried alone.

The memories of my childhood are otherwise pleasant. My family's abundance of love was enough to carry me through the other comparatively mundane pangs of growing up. I have always spoken about the two gifts my parents gave me: work ethic and faith. My father's work ethic knew no bounds and my mother's faith always gave the family hope. These were two gifts that would need to keep on giving in order to meet the challenges of our voyage to the United States.

2. The Voyage

We were poor. Of course, as a child I had no idea this was the case. My parents sheltered us in more ways than one within a three-hundred-square-foot, two-room house in Mexico City. All seven of us—three brothers, a sister, Mom, Dad, and myself—were literally quite close. We slept in one room that contained three beds. The second room did triple duty as dining room, living room, and kitchen. We made sure to squeeze the potential out of each square foot and, with no remaining space, the bathroom went where it logically could fit: outside. I was five when the house seemingly came to life, shaking as water pumped through its pipes for the first time. As we continued to grow, so did the house, creaking as it reached its full maturation with the addition of a tiny kitchen and small bathroom. The conveniences of a telephone, refrigerator, and car—which I now take for granted—existed only in the realm of fiction.

And, we counted ourselves among the lucky. My grandfather had given my dad a plot of land to build our two-room abode, along with two additional separate rooms that we rented out. My dad's salary from working at Byron

Jackson (a water pump factory) coupled with the rent money was just enough for us to live from week to week. For my dad, this meant, come rain or shine, he was out the door by five-thirty A.M. six days a week, with Saturday being a half-day. Every morning, my mom would rise before him to make his coffee. They tried as hard as they could not to wake us, but that proved difficult with everyone sleeping in the same room. No matter what, even when sick, my dad would force himself to go to work. It was a simple formula, really: one missed day of work equaled one evening with seven empty plates on the dinner table.

My mom made the best of our situation and never let on how much we were truly struggling. There was only enough money for the real necessities: food, water, electricity, and gas. Every now and then we bought an article of clothing, but mostly our wardrobes consisted of hand-me-downs from our aunts and ourselves. Each one of us had exactly two pairs of shoes—one fancy pair for school and church and the other for daily wearing. We never needed shoes for events like dining out because the farthest we went to satisfy our palates was to a lady in the neighborhood who sold food outside her house on Friday and Saturday nights. But somehow, my mom managed to make that trip seem like an adventure whose reward was an almost forbidden pleasure. What made those outings so special was that my mom would choose only one of her children to accompany her on her errands. When it was my turn, she'd pull me aside and furtively whisper, "Because you've been such a good girl, I'm going to treat you to your choice of a pozole, tostada, or taco." The first bite always beamed me up to childhood heaven. The ear-to-ear smile on my mom's face said it all: she was content to see us enjoying food that she did not have to cook. I'm certain that she re-created the adventure with each of my siblings, but by taking us one at a time, she made each of us feel special. In retrospect, I know that the sad truth is that she could not afford to treat all her children at once. Today, as a mother myself, I can fully appreciate the lengths she went to in order to make sure we felt like the center of her universe.

As time wore on, I noticed that our culinary adventures started to dwindle and eventually the childhood illusion that we were doing okay began to dissipate. What remained was a grimmer reality. The walls of our house seemed to be closing in on us. There wasn't enough money to make needed repairs. My parents' faces grew longer. It became obvious that something needed to be done to remedy our situation, and soon. Any way we sliced it, my dad's salary was simply not enough. My mom taught catechism and managed the household, but that didn't pay the bills. My parents knew that even if they continued to make enough to just get by, the future still looked bleak. Staying in Mexico would mean that we couldn't afford to extend our education beyond the ninth grade. Like most people we knew, we'd have to start working immediately. The vicious cycle of financial despondency would continue. We were in dire straits, and like millions before us, we decided to seek out a better life by embarking on a voyage that, at the very least, gave hope for a better life.

The Pursuit of Happiness

It was 1969 and I was an eleven-year-old being torn from her father. My parents decided that it would be best if my dad went to the United States first before we made the commitment to transplant the whole family. His *compadre* (close friend) Eusebio Peralta had been in the U.S. for a few years and was, after a short time, able to bring over the rest of his family; the expectation was that my dad would do the same. He'd live with the Peralta family who had previously rented from us in Mexico and, eventually, save up enough money working at a factory that embroidered labels to rent a place spacious enough for the entire family. A few days before my dad was scheduled to leave us, I saw mixed emotions manifest themselves on his face. While he was excited about a new beginning, the weight of not being able to see his family for at least a year was becoming harder to bear as the day of his departure approached.

Even though we knew he was leaving, when the day actually arrived, it was still shocking. A constant stream of people flowed through our house to bid him farewell. At first it felt like any other gathering, but soon the two rooms of our house looked as though they'd burst at the seams. Each additional person who arrived made his imminent departure more concrete. While we knew of people who had moved to the States, no one from our family had done it before. It involved a certain amount of unsettling risk.

Although the spotlight was on my dad that day, my mom's presence was heard, her feet shuffling over the concrete floor. Always the perfect hostess, she busied her hands with making sure guests' needs were attended to; she must have known that pausing for too long would invite someone to rope her into a conversation that could lead to choking back tears. Surely this was a sacrifice worth making . . . right?

Then the inevitable happened: it was time to take my dad to the bus depot. Thoughts buzzed menacingly around me: *What if we never see him again? What if the bus has an accident? What if he forgets about us?* We knew some men who abandoned their families after falling for some other woman in the U.S., forgetting about their previous life as though it were a bad dream. Surely my dad could never do such a thing. I tried to muster up the right combination of words that would change his mind about leaving and keep us together as a family. I hugged him as strongly as I could and told him we'd wait for him. A chorus of crying erupted with my mom as the leading soprano. Any emotional restraint that had been exercised earlier was gone; people began to stare and nod their heads knowingly. The discord of pain made it clear that we had never said good-bye to a loved one. The bus engine roared, coughed, and then enveloped us in its exhaust. The plan was for my dad to visit in a year, which for a child is like saying that you'll never see your dad again.

Although I knew he had left, I half expected to see my dad the following morning. I had hoped that as soon as the bus pulled away, he'd realize that moving to the U.S. was an ill-conceived plan. He'd tap the bus driver's shoulder and demand that he turn the infernal metallic beast around.

That morning, the bathroom mirror surprised me with a reflection of a blotchy blowfish that bore only slight resemblance to me—evidence that the previous day's crying and what brought it about were real. Our mother's brothers (our uncles), sensing that we might need emotional support during my dad's absence, began to visit more often. Sometimes we'd accidentally call them *Papi,* Dad, and immediately correct ourselves. Where there had once been my dad, there was now an uneasy silence that we carefully stepped around. We now take the technologies that keep us in touch for granted. In 1970s Mexico, we had no telephone, no e-mail, no fax machine. Postal mail acted as a lifeline to our dad. A new ritual replaced the early-morning routine of my mom preparing coffee for my dad. Now, my mom planted herself in front of the window, waiting patiently for the postman. The hope of any news from my dad was what kept us going. Soon, like clockwork every other Friday, we expected a handwritten letter whose unfolding revealed a check that got us through the next two weeks. Although we ate plentifully on those days, no amount of food could substitute for my dad. We'd often talk about him and imagine what his days were like and speculate about our future in another country. We prayed for his healthy return. Each bite was filled with gratitude for my dad who, even from afar, was able to put food on the table.

There was no denying that we were financially better off than when my dad was in Mexico. The money that he was earning was enough for him to live in the U.S. and for us to enjoy a higher standard of living in Mexico. The emotional cost of the move, however, was wearing on my mom, who was left to raise five children on her own while profoundly missing my dad.

His homecoming a year later will forever be etched in my memory. We had missed him so much and his arrival eased our minds. Like past explorers, he returned bearing exotic riches: clusters of clothes, throngs of toys, and stacks of Wrigley's spearmint gum. He offered me a piece of gum and I chewed it for hours until it became a flavorless mass and my jaw ached. With his savings, we were able to go on our first family vacation. I was twelve years old, and as far as I was concerned, life couldn't have been better.

We inundated our dad with questions about his new life. Sadly, sometimes when addressing him, we'd slip and call him *tío,* uncle, and quickly attempt to correct ourselves by calling him *Papi,* Dad. It was embarrassing for everyone. He'd pretend not to notice, but we knew that our slips of tongue lacerated his face like tiny whips. A year away from a growing child is equivalent to many more, as I, too, would later find out. Despite our best efforts, there was a widening rift forming between us. Even though he was physically present, we had never felt more distant from our dad. We needed to be together again as a family. My dad described the beauty of California and its calming sun. He tapped his thumbs against his chest, proclaiming: "I'm proof of how many opportunities we'll have if we work hard." It was a done deal. Plans for our move were set into motion. My dad would return to Mexico to work through the piles of paperwork necessary to uproot a family. If all went smoothly, we'd be reunited in a year.

But . . . Wait!

I was doing very well in school. Other than not having my dad with me, I couldn't have been happier, surrounded by my friends and cousins. I couldn't imagine leaving them. And what about my grandmother? What was I going to do in a country that was not mine? How would I learn English? The question marks pounded into my gut and left me breathless. And of course, the daily double question remained: What about my Quinceañera?

From an early age, every girl in Mexico dreams about what her Quinceañera will be like. I was no exception. It's a lavish event that celebrates a girl's turning fifteen and entering into womanhood; it's similar to a debutante's coming-out party. I had played through even the smallest details in my mind, orchestrated the whole affair. It began—as was the custom—with a mariachi band serenading me in front of my house the night before the celebration. The next morning I'd step into a most beautiful full-length white gown, carefully place my matching headdress upon my head, and gingerly hold the beautiful bouquet that had been prepared especially for the occasion. Then onto the church with my parents, godparents, and members of my court, consisting of carefully chosen young women and men. It's a beautiful ceremony that ends with placing my bouquet on the altar. And just when I thought the day couldn't get any better, we'd skip off to a banquet hall for dinner and dancing. The highlights would be waltzing with my dad, followed by his long toast to me. There is a wonderful predictability to the rite of passage that, as a Mexican girl, I felt entitled to. It was settled in my mind: we would not go to the U.S. until after my Quinceañera.

Unfortunately, I was just a child and certainly not the one laying down the rules. If events proceeded as planned, we'd leave in December of 1972; my Quinceañera would take place in August of the following year. I came up with possible solutions. The best one involved staying behind with family members in Mexico and having my parents come back to visit on my special day. Of course, I'd miss them, but it would be worth it. After my party they could take me anywhere they wanted, but not before. I was determined to have my Quinceañera dream become a reality. Meanwhile, planning for our departure was going along smoothly, and I secretly wished that something would happen to delay or maybe even cancel our trip. Representatives from my dad's company visited our house to help us fill out paperwork. We visited the Mexican Foreign Relations Department to get our passports (I'm sure I didn't smile for that picture), and then we were off to the U.S. embassy for our visas. My optimism for our staying in Mexico began to fade.

But then came a faint glimmer of hope during a meeting with the U.S. consul. She informed my mom that there was no way green cards could be issued to all her children because my dad didn't earn enough money to support the entire family. My immediate reaction was excitement, followed quickly by disbelief. It didn't make sense. For the past year, my dad had been making enough money to support himself in the U.S. and us in Mexico. I honestly thought we were rolling in money. My mom tried to convince the consul that we could make it on my dad's salary. We knew how to stretch an American dollar. My mom promised to start working as soon as her feet touched U.S. soil. The consul was unrelenting, shaking her head no to each suggestion. My mom wrung her hands in response, cried, and begged her not to tear our family apart once again. The consul, while seemingly touched, threw her hands up. "Four green cards, that's my best offer, nothing else I can do." The green cards would be distributed among my mother, my older brother Fernando, my little sister Margarita, and myself. My mom's two youngest children, my two brothers Mariano and Daniel, would stay behind. The plan was for my mom, my brother, and myself to earn the additional income to meet the minimum requirements for my two brothers to join us as soon as possible.

Once we arrived home, I set into motion my own plan by suggesting that I stay behind in Mexico to take care of my two younger brothers, aged ten and twelve. This would grant my mom peace of mind and allow me to celebrate my Quinceañera. Could the plan be any more perfect? My mom didn't seem to think so, not even pausing to entertain my plan for a second. She agreed with the consul that it would be best if I worked a part-time job in the U.S. in order to have the family reunited sooner. "Don't forget that you're a girl, Rosario, and you need more protection than your brothers," she often reminded me. Now as a mother myself, I can only imagine the strength it took for my mom to choose among her children. It was a decision no mother should ever have to make. It was clearly killing her on the inside. As our departure date approached, there was a shift in plans. My older brother would stay behind to look after my two younger brothers. I tried to hide how jealous I was of Fernando's staying in Mexico. I didn't want to make this any more difficult than it already was for my mom. In the end, the three women of the family were to take the voyage.

Everything was, sadly, set. The end of December 1972 was our departure date. This would allow us to start a new year in a new country in a new school. Everything we had known and loved our entire lives would be left behind. The timing couldn't have been any more painful. In Mexico we celebrate nine days of *posadas* leading up to Christmas and then, like the entire world, we celebrate New Year's. These were festivities that everyone looked forward to all year long. I wanted my mom to leave me behind. I cried. I begged. I began to lose hope. My mom, while understanding, assured me that I'd make new friends, that it would be worth it when I saw how much better our life would be. I tried to explain that I didn't need an improved life. I didn't need new friends. I didn't need anything to change. My life was perfect as is. How could I leave my friends, cousins . . . and what about my grandma?

To this day, I can still play back my grandmother's departing words with great clarity: "Bless you my child. I trust that you'll continue to be an upright lady and make me proud." Her eyes that day were bloodshot from crying and her face contorted in anguish. She ordered me to never veer from our family values and to stay in school, succeed, and ensure that this sacrifice was not in vain. She prayed with me, asking the Virgen de Guadalupe (the symbolic mother of Mexicans) to guide and shield me with her *manto sagrado,* her sacred gown. My grandmother hugged me tightly, wrapping me in her shawl, and then slowly unraveled me into an uncertain future. I wept loudly while trying not to think about things like how much longer she would "be" with us. Of course, at the time, I didn't stop to think about how difficult it was for my mom to be leaving her mom. Over the years, the two of them had worked as a team to raise us. They did such a great job that I never realized how poor and limited our resources were. They had given us so much love and attention that it made up for whatever material wealth we may have lacked. I guess when you aren't aware of what you don't have, you can't exactly miss it. But even then, my grandma and my mom had instilled a sense of fate in us and this was in the plan, and, as painful as it seemed, it was meant to be.

And then, like a recurring nightmare, we were at the bus depot again. This time we were the ones leaving. It turned out that it was even more difficult then being the ones left behind. I imagined that this must've been what my dad had felt when he left us. This time the metallic beast would carry us in its belly. By the time of our actual departure, I was an emotional zombie, unable to cry anymore. It was as though my tear ducts had shriveled and refused to express what I was feeling. No amount of tears could change events, so what was the point? My three brothers waved good-bye; my grandma waved good-bye; my cousins waved good-bye. I'll never forget the flurry of hands, the quivering of lips, and the feeling of vertigo that overtook me as our bus pulled away from the depot.

The next two days of our voyage to Tijuana went by with

painful slowness. I'd wake up and go back to sleep and somehow we were still on the bus. Drifting in and out of consciousness, I never bothered to see if it was day or night. My sister and I played games, but we soon tired of them. Time suspended, leaving me to dangle alone in an abyss, heavy with my thoughts. I imagined the *posadas* leading up to New Year's. Before drifting off to sleep, my mind would always arrive at the same summoned scene of my Quinceañera, the party of all parties, the party I resigned myself to never having. The ceaseless bus engine lulled me to sleep again and again—until I awoke to a new vista.

A Whole New World

My mom yawned loudly, tearing me away from the flashing scenery outside the window. The weariness of the two-day voyage was evident on my mom's and sister's faces. Then it hit me: we'd soon see my dad. I had been so absorbed in the emotional turmoil of leaving Mexico that I forgot we would be reunited with him.

And what a reunion it was! My dad met us at the bus depot in Tijuana and hand-in-hand we walked across the border to catch a Greyhound bus to our new home. I was happy to see my dad alive and well (and slightly plumper, too).

I rubbed my eyes as we crossed the border and entered the freeway. The same sun that had bathed California gold rushers crossing the border in the 1800s greeted us upon our arrival in California on December 22, 1972—just two days prior to Christmas Eve. Breaking free from the traffic of the border, our bus reflected sunlight and must've looked like a shiny silver bullet. All around me, everything looked serene, beautiful, and clean. The sharp edges of the scenery popped with luminous colors. My senses came back to life after two days of mostly listening to the hum of a bus engine and the occasional hiccup of wheels hitting a bump in the road. I was in a new country; my senses were on high alert. The only thing that was certain was that everything was different. The distraction of my new surroundings was a welcome change after two days of living within the stuffy confines of my head.

I couldn't help but be distracted by what I saw when we opened the door of his apartment in Huntington Park. I stepped into what looked like a luxury apartment built sometime in the distant future. Surely this wasn't *my* dad's place. How could he afford everything I saw around me? There would be time for questions later. My sister and I joined hands and bounded over a couch. Our legs after the two days of bus-seat contortion couldn't have felt more free if they had been wings. We left my parents in each other's arms while we explored a fully furnished, fully assembled, fully unexplored apartment. It looked like a stage set for The Brady Bunch—which we would certainly be able to watch on one of the two color television sets! I lifted a phone from its receiver and heard a dial tone. I must have been holding it for some time because the operator came on and spoke in a language I didn't understand. I turned on the kitchen sink knobs to wash my hands and almost burned myself with the water. How was this possible if no one had turned on a boiler? In the U.S. I found we could turn on any faucet and hot water would gush forth; if that wasn't incredible enough, we no longer needed to buy gas tanks for the stove. There was a large refrigerator filled with food. All around me were gizmos I had yet to tinker with. Everything was geared toward making cooking easy, convenient, and comfortable. I also found that I was nice and toasty, although it was a bit chilly outside. My dad, amused by my wonderment, explained that a heater kept the apartment at a comfortable temperature, even during the winter. I lamentably imagined my brothers and grandma bundled in blankets in Mexico.

Once the newness of the apartment wore off, just two days later, we celebrated our first Christmas in California. It was awful. My dad's coworker invited us to her family's home to spend Christmas Eve. It was a *very* small gathering. We met a handful of strangers and tried to make the best of it. Back home the gathering would have numbered at least thirty family members—a true fiesta that led up to a midnight mass. I may have been physically present in California that night, but my heart was in Mexico.

New Year's was just as bad; in fact it, was worse. It was my little brother Mariano's eleventh birthday and not being in Mexico to celebrate it with him made the reality of our new life painfully obvious. At the very least, I hoped he was having a better time than I was in the U.S. I felt so vulnerable, emotionally stripped down, and, for the first time in my life, I was suddenly shy. As much as I tried to keep an open mind, I missed Mexico. I resisted resignation, but as time wore on it came thundering along. There was no way around it, this was my new life and there was nothing I could do to change that. I had to accept this new reality in order to move on. I mourned leaving Mexico by alternating between weeping ceaselessly during the day and muffling my cries in a pillow at night. I didn't want my parents to feel any more guilt. They couldn't stand to see the anguish I was going through and, even when I tried to hide it, my mom knew that I was not okay.

One night I was quietly weeping when my mom peeled me from my pillow. "I don't know exactly how, but we'll return to Mexico for your Quinceañera," she said, wiping away my tears. "I promise you, *mi'jita,* you'll have your day." I tried to say that it wasn't necessary, that I'd be okay, but my mom has always been able to see through me. When she insisted, I couldn't help but smile. It was a huge sacrifice that required both of my parents to work overtime to afford four round-trip tickets to Mexico and, of course, the celebration itself.

I slept soundly that night. It was only after my mom made that promise that I felt I could take a deep breath and begin my life in this new country. The days didn't seem so torturous, knowing that I'd be reunited with all of my family and friends in six months. With each passing day, my anticipation grew.

School Days

The culture shock began with the clattering of the school bell. My parents knew that an education in the U.S. would

be the key to their children's success. Our education was one
of the main reasons we left Mexico and my parents stressed
the importance of making them proud. If anything could
rival the feeling of disbelief when I entered our U.S. apartment, it was the grandiosity of my new junior high school. I
imagined this school looking down at my former school,
tapping it on the head as though it were its small foreign
cousin. I was beginning the ninth grade even though I had
already completed it months ago in Mexico. At that time,
you were placed in a grade based solely on your age. Since I
wasn't fifteen yet, I'd have to attend the last semester of
junior high school.

Oddly enough, it looked as though everything inside was
gratis, from the food at lunch to school supplies to books. I
thought it strange, but I didn't want to mention anything. I
thought that they might make my parents pay for everything. In Mexico, only elementary school books were free;
after that everything came at a hefty price. Here, not only
was the food free; but it was delicious. Even after all these
years, I can still taste the coffee cake, pizza, and fish sticks.
The books and the writing paper were of the best quality;
rarely did they rip when I made an erasure.

Since I didn't know anyone, I was free to fully absorb my
surroundings. And what I saw appalled me. I saw student
after student line up to throw out food that they had barely
touched. Unopened chocolate milk cartons met the same
fate. Sometimes, after making a silly error, an entire sheet of
paper was crumpled and thrown out. What kind of country
was this where students threw away food and supplies that
my parents couldn't afford to pay for? How could my class-

mates be so ungrateful? Not only could I not believe my eyes, but my ears must have been playing tricks on me, too. In more than one class, I heard students get angry and actually talk back to teachers. Students wouldn't even think about doing something so disrespectful in Mexico, unless they were eager to be punished by teachers and parents. And what was everyone wearing? I was accustomed to seeing male teachers donning coat and tie and female teachers with high heels and makeup. Didn't these people care about the way they presented themselves? Some teachers even showed up in T-shirts and sandals. It became obvious that it was okay for students to not comb their hair or iron their pants. I had worn a uniform during the past nine years and would never dare to leave the house with wrinkled clothing and disheveled hair. As a newcomer, I was looking for the security of rules that didn't seem to exist. Even for parties, people stayed in their jeans. In my family, every outing merited skirts, jackets, and ties. Since we so seldom went to parties, my parents dressed us up to go to the movies. In the theater, swarms of people clad in jeans and shorts surrounded us. We stuck out like sore thumbs. And not just in the theater, for that matter; the whole country seemed so casual. If anything was certain, it was that we weren't in Kansas—err, Mexico—any longer.

The dark underbelly of life both inside and outside of school was soon exposed. Classmates younger than myself—mostly Chicano boys and girls—were already in gangs. Their traditional garb included: khakis or jeans that were at least five sizes too big, white T-shirts covered by plaid flannel shirts (often rolled up strategically to show off tattoos), and hickies that formed bruised necklaces. I could only imagine what my dad would have done if I had ever come home with anything that even resembled a hickie. To make sure we didn't stray from the course, my dad wasn't above using scare tactics by describing things he had seen not only on television, but with his own eyes: gang killings, drugs, crime, and prostitution. Things that may have existed in Mexico, but we had never seen.

Our response was to cling together. The collective learning curve was steep. Being in the same boat, as it were, we grew even stronger as a family. Although we were not a complete family with my brothers back in Mexico, the four of us knew that we could rely on one another. Even when my little sister and I would have a fight, we'd still walk to and from school together. For that matter, we did everything together.

Life began to settle into some semblance of a routine. Monday through Friday flew by with classes, homework, and cleaning the house. And the weekends came to be what we lived for. On Saturdays, my sister and I would make sure that the entire apartment was spotless and our homework was complete before my parents arrived home from work. Our reward: eating out at a restaurant! Sundays were even better. The only day my parents didn't work began with a mile-long walk to catch a bus that would drop us off thirty minutes later in downtown Los Angeles. Once there, we'd attend Spanish mass at the church of La Placita Olvera. It was comforting to end the week with a mass spoken in Spanish, after being besieged by English all week. I also found that I was able to connect to the same God I prayed to in Mexico. I prayed for a lot of things back then, but mostly for the safe reunion of our family.

After filing out of church, we'd head over to Clifton's Cafeteria, our mouths already watering with anticipation. The first time we ate there, my mouth dropped in awe. I had never been to a buffet-style restaurant. The food was endless and tantalizing. Rest would not come until my palate had tasted every possible food. "It's okay, Rosario. Get whatever and as much as you want," my dad said, amused at my disbelief. *These Americans sure know how to eat,* I thought. Determined to stretch my family's dollars as far as they could go, I loaded up my plate. My arms trembled under the weight of my tray. I rolled up my sleeves, looked across from me, and saw that my dad had a simple chicken breast in the center of his plate. It was a typical case of my eyes having a more voracious appetite than my belly. I was unable to finish my food and asked my dad to help me out because I felt bad about throwing food away. My dad also helped out my sister with her overburdened plate. I buffed my satisfied belly and stared down at it like a large crystal ball that showed the past, when electrifying excitement would flood through me, knowing it was my turn to visit the neighborhood lady who sold pozoles, tostadas, and tacos outside her home. How quickly life could change.

But then there were the times when we were just about to dig in and there would be an eerie silence, the clinking of our silverware amplified. My mom hesitated and a few bites into her meal would start crying, a lump of food getting caught in her throat. This would strike randomly and often, both at home and in restaurants. "How could I just sit here and eat when your *hermanos* could be starving?" she'd ask the table. Of course, it was always difficult to eat after that. We'd slowly and sheepishly fork food into our mouths.

Communication with my brothers in Mexico was as slow as carrier pigeons and as helpless as smoke signals. The patience and planning required seems unimaginable in today's electronically connected world. There were no cell phones or e-mail in the 1970s. If we wanted to keep in touch, we had to set pen to paper. It would often take at least two weeks for our letters to arrive in Mexico. If we wanted to speak with my brothers, we had to specify the date, time, and phone number where we'd call them. This was required because international phone calls were absurdly expensive and my family didn't even own a phone in Mexico. To be on the safe side, we sent our letters at least three weeks ahead of the appointed day of the phone call. It wasn't rare for letters to arrive later than usual. To say the least, our communication with my brothers was very limited.

My mom was able to find some consolation in knowing that she'd see her children in a few months when we returned for my Quinceañera. Looking back, I wonder how she was able to bear not seeing her sons for months. When I studied the lines of my mom's face, I saw hints of her underlying sadness, indications that suffering and motherhood were intertwined. We did grow more upbeat as the day of our return to Mexico approached. We looked forward to seeing my brothers and grandma again.

The Big Day

Looking back, I realize how simple my Quinceañera was and how much I relied on my imagination to fill in the blanks to create a day that looked and felt exactly like the day I had dreamily rehearsed in my mind's eye. My dress—a bit too small in some areas and bunched up in others—was off a sale rack at Lerner's. I'm sure my parents ran out of money because, instead of a fresh bouquet of flowers, I carried a hastily assembled arrangement of plastic flowers wrapped in a bakery napkin. And I couldn't have been happier. The dress might as well have been designed by Gucci and the bouquet a kaleidoscope of exotic flowers. This was *my* dress, *my* bouquet, *my* party, *my* day. And I could smile if I wanted to! I was beaming through the incessant rain of that day. Luckily, the sky cleared just in time for the six P.M. mass and reception filled with food and dancing. It was an unforgettable evening for me. I danced and twirled with guests until I was ready to collapse. On my face was a permanently plastered smile. I felt an overwhelming sense of gratitude toward my parents for making sure I experienced this rite of passage. They had made me feel like Cinderella; I was determined to show them how grateful I was by honoring their sacrifices. After my Quinceañera, I felt like I had put in place the remaining piece of the puzzle and could now return to the U.S. with my mission accomplished.

Back to School

I knew that the best way to repay my parents for the trip to Mexico was to excel in school. At that time, every student entering the tenth grade had to take an intelligence quotient test. An average IQ was set at one hundred points. My score was twenty-seven, a number I'll never forget because it landed on my desk with a thump of a teacher's stubby finger, circled in red. The point was made crystal clear with a degrading chuckle. The students took this as a go-ahead to also laugh at me. The classroom was lively with echoing laughter. I was not amused. Surprisingly, I didn't respond with anger or sadness. I knew that the only thing the test proved was that I didn't know the language it was written in. The message was clear: I needed to learn English, and quickly. That classroom filled with laughter was exactly what I'd use to fuel my efforts. I knew I was more intelligent than the IQ test would have everyone believe. I embarked on an English media diet that consisted of reading daily newspapers, listening to radio, and watching the news. Initially, I had no idea what newscasters were saying, and the newspapers may have just as well been written in Braille. Slowly, however, with the help of photos and videos, I began to understand more and more. To verify my comprehension, I tuned to channel thirty-four (the only Spanish-language station) and saw that I was grasping more each day. My progress was coming along slowly but surely.

At school, I doubled and then tripled my efforts. I was diligent about completing every homework and extra-credit assignment. All my efforts culminated in graduating from high school with honors. Although that was the school's official confirmation of my efforts, it didn't trump the time a U.S.-born student asked me how to spell the word *beautiful*. On the bottom of my high school diploma was a gold star acknowledging my good grades, and the local Rotary Club gave me a fifty-dollar savings bond for perfect attendance. It never occurred to me to miss school, even when I felt a bit sick. I had grown up watching my dad rise before the sun each morning to head to work. Although it may have been that my unflagging attendance was motivated more by fear than determination. I was convinced that the one day I was absent, the teacher would present a critical piece of information that I needed for a test.

In the meantime, my older brother had joined the family in the U.S.—along with my two younger brothers—and was able to graduate with the class of 1976, at the same time as me. My parents were so proud that their two older children were on their way to achieving the American Dream. We had been through twice the amount of school as our parents by graduating from high school. Having only an elementary education themselves, they felt that their job with us was through, that we could make it out there. I'll never forget the sound of my dad's voice trembling with pride, providing a soundtrack for our graduation video. More than anything else I know he was very proud of himself. After all, he took his children's achievements to be his own.

Due to our economic situation at home, upon graduation, the family decided that I'd get a full-time job, while my brother attended college full-time. My baby sister Nancy had been born two years earlier, and it was difficult for my parents to take care of her while holding down full-time jobs. If I went to work, it would allow my mom to stay home and take care of the baby while running the household. I know what you're thinking: *How unfair!* At the time I didn't see it that way. It was the 1970s and I had been raised in a Catholic Mexican immigrant family. I wouldn't have dared to broach the topic of equal rights with my parents. Yes, there was a double standard, but that's just the way it was. The main governing principle was simple: you are part of this family, so you will contribute with whatever is needed for its survival. You don't ask questions. Oh, and don't forget to smile. Seriously, it was no problem at all. I was happy to do my part for the family. My parents' rationale was that as a woman I'd be provided for once I got married. It followed logically that there was no need for a college education, since a man would provide for me. On the other hand, my brother was on the other side of that arrangement and would have to take on the duty of providing for his future wife and family.

I had a plan. During the summers, I had kept busy working for the city of Huntington Park under a federal program called the Comprehensive Employment and Training Act that offered paid positions to high school students. I learned about the way the city functioned from the inside by working in its various departments: building, planning, and the city administrator's office. Typically, the CETA program was only available to high school students for two summers and once students graduated, they were no longer eligible. Over the course of the two years I worked for it, I had built a reputation for being a hard worker who was always on time and could be relied on. There was a secretary named Moanne who took a liking to me and convinced the city manager's office to make an exception and allow me to work with them since I wasn't eighteen yet. After some discussion, I was able to work one more summer there after my high school graduation. When the fall came, Mr. Fogel, the city personnel manager, helped me find my first job. He sung my praises to managers at Barth & Dreyfus, a towel company in Vernon, Los Angeles. A few weeks later, I was a shipping clerk.

I began to make enough money for my mom to leave her job and stay home with my baby sister. I decided that in addition to my full-time job, I'd take night classes at East Los Angeles College. I couldn't believe that after only being in the United States a few years, I was going to college. For the four years I went to that college, I don't think my mom stopped worrying about my safety. I could still hear her plaintive pleas: "What if your car breaks down? Or worse, someone attacks you in the parking lot? What if, what if . . ." There were still no cell phones to act as mother pacifiers. Knowing that she would not be able to sleep until I arrived, I rushed home after my classes, usually arriving around ten-thirty P.M. I tried my best not to run late because I knew she'd be racked with worry. She'd only budge from her spot at the window once she saw my Ford Maverick's headlights peer around our street's corner. She'd proceed to make her way to the kitchen to heat up my dinner, her silhouette trailing behind.

I worked for Barth & Dreyfus for a couple of years before

taking a secretarial position with a mortgage banking company. After a few months and with a growing hunger for advancement in the company, I asked my boss which classes I should take to help me climb the ladder. He thought for a quick moment and suggested a few shorthand and secretarial classes. When I gently suggested that I wanted to be more than a secretary, it became clear that no matter how hard I tried, he'd always see me as a secretary. I left after working there for only a few months.

Meanwhile, my sister Margarita had been working for Getty Oil. Within the same building was the trust accounting department of Union Bank. One of her friends knew a woman from the bank, and they were looking for someone who could quickly type numbers. I applied for that position and got it on the spot. I ended up working in that department for about a year and a half when, out of the blue, I received a call from a headhunter. She asked if I'd be interested in applying for a receptionist position with City National Bank. There was a lot to consider: although I'd be taking a step down in position, I'd be taking a step up in salary. Plus, the headhunter assured me that if I did well, I would benefit from the bank's policy of promoting from within. Opportunities for advancement were severely lacking in my two former positions, and I knew that, if given the chance, I'd rise. Although I'd have to once again work hard to prove myself, I decided to take the position.

How far a step down it was became crystal clear during one of my first days of work. Another receptionist who sat right next to me and had been training me was nowhere to be found. The volume of calls coming in was so high that it required two receptionists, our desks side-by-side. The phone was ringing. After some hesitation, I lifted it from its cradle and began to diligently take the caller's message. The voice on the other end of the line asked for my name and title. I told him my name and said that I was the receptionist. My colleague tapped my shoulder indignantly and said, "No, actually, *I'm* the receptionist!" I apologized to the caller on the other end of the line and quickly corrected myself: "Excuse me, sir, I'm the assistant to the receptionist." I have always treasured that memory because it gives me a clear sense of where I began.

Despite this rough start, taking the position at the bank was the best decision I could've made. The headhunter was right: I worked hard, and they in turn promoted me almost every six months. I continued to attend classes at night and the management admired my determination to improve myself. My mom could see the toll that working so hard both at the bank and in school was taking on me. One day she lifted my face by the chin, looked into my droopy eyes, and innocently asked, *"¿Ay mi'jita, pa' que vas a la escuela si ya eres secretaria en un banco . . . y en Beverly Hills?"* "Oh my dear child, why do you still need to go to school when you are a secretary in a bank *and* in Beverly Hills?" My mom couldn't see what all the fuss was about. I tried to remind myself that she only had an elementary-school education. From her perspective, I had already made it. I had achieved more than she could ever imagine for herself. She'd brag to friends and family that I worked in posh Beverly Hills. It was then that I realized I was not seeking my parents' or managers' approval. No, I wanted to prove to a much harsher critic that I had what it took. I was guided by an internal hunger to succeed that simply would not rest. I hugged my mom and told her that although I was happy to be a secretary for now, the only way I would continue to rise was if I attained a higher degree. She had been thinking that once I finished my two-year degree at ELAC, it would be the end of my education. It had taken me four long years to attain a two-year degree, but I was nowhere near finished. When I told my mom that I needed to go to a university, her eyes rolled.

I never looked back; I just kept going. I didn't even see the point in attending the graduation ceremony at ELAC. I transferred over the summer to California State University of Los Angeles. That would take me three more years to complete. Seven years after high school I graduated with my B.S. in business administration and marketing from Cal State. Again, I didn't attend the graduation ceremony because I didn't see any cause for celebration. Attaining an M.B.A.—that would be something worthy of celebration.

When I left the bank six years later in 1986, "assistant" was close to being in my title again, but this time it would have been as an assistant vice president. My hard-earned promotion, however, would not come to pass. It turned out that my long workdays at the bank coupled with night classes would pale in comparison to the challenges of motherhood.

3. Life B.E. and A.E.

In 1985, before I left my position at the bank, my husband Alex and I were intoxicated with impending parenthood. Everything was set to welcome Eric into our home. Baby room decorated in blue? Check. Piles of fluffy baby clothes folded neatly? Check. Hospital bag packed for the past two weeks? Check. Everything was proceeding according to plan. Life was good. My family waited in anticipation.

September, it turns out, is a busy month for hospital delivery rooms; as a low-risk mother it was decided that I'd give birth to Eric at a hospital a bit farther out in Downey. Once my contractions began, we called the hospital and my family. I was having a baby! Finally, the precious being that had lived inside me for nine months would reveal his perfect self.

When we arrived at the hospital, I was immediately placed in a preliminary exam room. With my knees propped up and legs spread wide, the head nurse began to check my cervix to approximate how long labor would be. Then, mid-exam, the nurse emerged wide-eyed from in between my legs and bounded toward the wall, arms outstretched as though ready to take flight. She tapped a red button like an

41

impatient elevator rider. And with that, I felt as though I had left my body to float around the room. I watched the scene below swirl around me as though it were straight out of a television medical drama. An army of six hospital staff arrived and busied themselves with their respective roles. An oxygen mask was sealed around my mouth, while the upper portion of the bed was slammed down.

"This baby is not getting enough oxygen, people!" the nurse said. "I can't get a heartbeat. Someone call a doctor and fast!"

The doctor arrived and quickly fired off questions. Then he said with equanimity, "Okay everyone, prep for a C-section."

"Just get the baby out. Don't worry about me. Don't let anything happen to him!" I repeated—my distressed mantra. The doctor reminded me to take deep breaths.

Moments later I heard my baby's first cry of liberation. Thank God. I took a deep breath and then it hit me like a boulder; the epidural anesthesia had worn me out. I raised my right eyelid with all my remaining strength in an attempt to catch a glimpse of my precious Eric being cleaned up by the huddled mass around him.

"I'm going to throw up," I said quietly before my eyelids dropped closed like a theater curtain.

Luckily I hadn't thrown up, although I couldn't move after regaining consciousness.

"I want to see my baby" were the first words that tumbled out of my mouth. The nurse asked me to wait a moment while she called in the pediatrician.

"My baby, please," I repeated when the pediatrician entered the room.

The pediatrician propped his clipboard on his hip. "That's not going to be possible, Ms. Marín." He ran his finger along the chart. "I'm sorry, but Eric is in critical condition and we're going to have to transfer him to the NIC in another hospital."

"What's wrong? Will he be okay?"

"We won't be sure of anything until we run some tests," he said. "Nothing's conclusive."

The doctor who delivered my baby interrupted the pediatrician and, perhaps noticing the look of anguish on my face, promised me that I'd be able to see Eric before they transferred him to the neonatal intensive care unit in the Kaiser Permanente Hospital. I was desperate to see my child. As the pediatrician continued to rattle off questions, all I could think about was holding my firstborn.

"Does anyone in your family have Asian-like features, Ms. Marín?"

"Well, my father is sometimes asked if he's Filipino." I thought how proud my father would be if the baby resembled him.

The pediatrician began to detail some of Eric's physical characteristics, which sounded like no one in my family. He then asked, "Does anyone in your family suffer from mental retardation?"

I grew faint. *What kind of question is that? Is this a joke? Why can't I just see my baby?*

"Have you ever heard of Down syndrome?"

Are you talking to me? My lower lip ached from my teeth baring down on it.

"I have a cousin who has Down syndrome. She's almost my age," I said. "Wait, are you implying that *my* son could have *that?*"

A nurse interrupted to let us know that an ambulance was already outside waiting to transfer Eric. As the doctor had promised, they brought Eric into my room. I tried to lift my head completely to get a clear view of him, but that proved difficult. Eric was boxed in an incubator, a tangle of tubes attached to his six-pound six-ounce body. With my remaining strength, I flung out my arm and tapped the incubator lightly as though it were a fish tank. I cried. I couldn't even hold my own son. I promised my baby that I'd join him soon.

"Do you think Eric has Down syndrome?" I asked the receiving doctor, wanting to extract the seed of doubt planted by the first pediatrician.

The doctor patted my shoulder and looked down at me with a puzzled expression. "I really don't think so because *those* children tend to be very lethargic and Eric is quite the busybody."

Those words gave me hope. They wheeled Eric away. As I lay alone in the hospital room, my mind began to race. The seeds of doubt sprouted within the darkest recesses of my brain. I couldn't take it anymore. I called my mom. Although she had been in the hospital during the delivery, she had left with everyone else after Eric was born. I gave her an update and mentioned the questions the pediatrician had asked me. I told her that I was in too much pain to go into the whole thing. I hung up the phone when she said that she was on the way to see me.

I had heard of the American expression of being on an emotional roller coaster, but I wondered what it meant exactly. After waiting four long days for the results of Eric's genetic tests, I began to wish I'd never heard of that cliché which somehow encompassed exactly what I was going through. I was happy that Eric was alive, but concerned over his ability to pull through. I was surrounded by family and yet often felt alone. There was a lot of dead air between my husband, Alex, and me as we resisted talking about all the what-ifs. We held hands and prayed that the genetic test results would return negative for Down syndrome. We were both going through similar feelings, but we worried about what would happen if we acknowledged them aloud in conversation. He, too, felt guilty, worried that he might not be able to fully embrace Eric if he had Down syndrome. Of course we felt that, regardless of the outcome, Eric had as much a right as anyone to be on earth. Unfortunately, I was bedridden for the first five days of Eric's life, but Alex visited our little boy every day in the intensive care unit. We made it a point to hold Eric as much as possible. Alex later admitted to me that he was more worried than he let on and had several conversations with relatives in search of reassurance that they'd accept Eric if it turned out that he did indeed have Down syndrome. I, too, was looking for reassurance. I'd search doctors' faces for hints about my son's condition; my emotions would rise and fall upon noticing even the slightest shift in facial muscles. I wanted answers, yet I dreaded asking questions. Imagine being on the most terrifying roller coaster you've ever been on. Now imagine what it would be like if you were strapped into it for four days straight. I still felt the highs and lows of the coaster's peaks and valleys, but I was almost completely numb: I was ready to get off that infernal ride.

The night before the genetic test results were due, the roller coaster began to rock violently. Over the past few days my family had been at my side, trying their best to distract me from my worries. We pretended the hospital food was actually tasty, relived past memories, and even cracked the occasional joke. We were having our last dinner at the hospital and were talking about anything other than the next day's test results. I felt some semblance of peace surrounded by loved ones. With their support, my husband and I might just be able to handle the next day's test results. The roller coaster began to ascend with our shared hope.

It was then that a female pediatrician came flying through the doorway: "Has anyone told you that your son has Down syndrome?"

After a long pause, my husband was the first to speak. "No, we're waiting for the test results to come in."

"I don't need genetic tests to tell me your son has Down syndrome. I can bet you he does."

With this doctor's lack of bedside manners, the emotional roller coaster made its final descent into a brick wall. My world felt like it was crumbling. In a split second, she had stripped us of the hope that had kept us going. All our prayers had fallen on deaf ears. I'll never find the words to describe the sea of feelings I was drowning in at that moment.

We told the pediatrician to go away; we had heard enough.

Her diagnosis of Down syndrome was confirmed the next day.

My mind raced: What would we do? Why me? Why us? What did we do to deserve such punishment? How could I face anyone? Sadness gave way to anger. Was this my reward for being a good daughter, sister, wife, and worker? Surely no one deserved this. I'm embarrassed to say that it was only after having this initial reaction that my thoughts turned to Eric. I was humbled and scared by the new questions that popped into my mind. What would become of Eric? What kind of life would he lead? Would there even be any sort of future for him? I lost any control over my thoughts as they leapt into a dismal abyss. What would happen to Eric if I died? Then all of a sudden, my own mortality was staring me in the face: I would die one day and most likely before he did. Oh my God, maybe it'd be better if he didn't make it at all. He was so ill that maybe it was in God's plan that he pass on to a better place. I could tell everyone that my baby was still-born. I'd never have to be ashamed of his mental retardation. I'd never have to explain his condition. I even went so far as to envision myself clad in a black dress for his funeral.

Then came the pangs of guilt. What kind of a mother would I be if I were having these thoughts? When my mind stopped, my heart kicked in. After all, this was *my* baby; I had carried him in my womb for nine months. His life, his survival, his happiness greatly depended on us, his parents. I had developed a loving relationship with this little being long before he decided it was time to show himself to the world. I had anxiously awaited his arrival and now he was here. He had looked so peaceful and beautiful as they wheeled him away. I didn't see the Down syndrome when I looked at his fragile body. I saw a baby—a baby that was mine. I was torn by the two extreme (and seemingly contradictory) emotions of love and rejection.

Luckily, help arrived in the form of Elise Sandiford. She was a great friend of ours and the only person, other than family, that I allowed to visit me in the hospital. As a special education teacher, Elise was able to help me put my feelings into perspective. With her nonjudgmental demeanor, she held my hand and detailed what I was going through.

"You're experiencing a natural grieving process: you're mourning the 'perfect' baby that you anticipated, while learning how to welcome Eric into your life."

I took a deep breath. Perhaps I shouldn't be so ashamed of what I was feeling.

"Anything you're feeling is not only okay, it's natural and human."

I'll always be indebted to Elise for her timely words. She validated my emotions and said that Eric could lead a very fruitful life. She explained that, with proper medical care and education, children with disabilities could be productive members of society. She brought me a couple of books about Down syndrome and provided us with other resources. With time, it began to seem manageable.

Eric stayed in the hospital for two weeks, in the neonatal intensive care unit. Every day we arrived as early as we could (promptly at seven A.M.) and stayed until they kicked us out at ten-thirty in the evening. The NICU was a flurry of activity at all hours—certainly not a peaceful place, surrounded by machine beeps and that unmistakable hospital smell. It often took two hours to feed Eric because he had to learn how to suck. We also needed to get him accustomed to a routine: feed him, change him, feed him, change him, bathe him, and lay him down to sleep. Oh, and when we could, we fit in our own meals.

Then one day a baby died. It was a painful realization that at any moment that could be my son. An unsettling macabre feeling of how much easier life would be if it had been my son seized me. I stuffed such thoughts down as far as I could. I was able to find peace in the hours spent watching Eric, studying his every slight movement. With time, I stopped noticing the physical characteristics of Down syndrome. Eric was perfect in my eyes and I swelled with a mother's pride.

A Breathless Realization

I lost it. Overtaken with pain and tears, I stampeded in frantic circles like a wounded and disoriented animal. I roared at the top of my lungs: "God, do not take my child! You've already given him to me! Please do not take him away now! I've accepted him as he is! I love him!" I steadied my finger to dial 911. Eric was six weeks old and not breathing. I was in the middle of feeding him when he stopped fidgeting. He froze completely. As if in slow motion, I saw my husband pinch Eric's nose and begin mouth-to-mouth resuscitation. I explained what was happening to the operator. The paramedics were dispatched. The wait was unbearable, the pain overwhelming, the entire event transformative.

Eric survived. This event marked the beginning of my new life. I fully accepted that Eric was a permanent part of my life. In his first five years, Eric would experience numerous health problems and face death five times. In order to be the best parents we could, we read anything and everything on Down syndrome. There was no Internet at that time, so we took out mountains of books from the library. My husband became the resident researcher. We figured that the more we knew, the greater Eric's chances of leading a full life.

We found out that the typical human has twenty-three pairs of chromosomes: one set from the female and the other from the male. From conception onward, people with Down syndrome have an extra, twenty-first chromosome (this means that rather than having a pair for the twenty-first chromosome, they have a third, extra chromosome attached)—a condition called Trisomy 21. This extra genetic material is responsible for the physical characteristics associated with Down syndrome: a short stature, mental retardation, and a flat-looking face. Because of their similarities, people with Down syndrome are sometimes said to have two families: their birth family and their Down syndrome family.

Then there is the whole slew of medical complications. In many cases, the five senses are compromised. With vision, for instance, Eric has nystagmus ("dancing eyes"), strabismus (crossed eyes), and myopia (nearsightedness). The majority of people with Down syndrome also have ear infections; some are even born with them. Eric had three double myringotomies (a procedure to drain ears). Speech problems are also common. Some, like Eric, are tactile defensive, which means their sense of touch is heightened. This expressed itself in Eric's fear of exploring the world around him. We'd do fun things like place his hands inside a bowl of spaghetti so that he would understand that it was safe to interact more actively with his surroundings. Many infants with Down syndrome are born with severe heart defects. Luckily Eric was spared those, but instead he had so many other medical problems. At birth, for instance, Eric had meconium aspiration, which caused his lungs to be fragile: a common cold would, and still does, last for months. Because of all this, we still make sure we take him to a doctor at the first hint of any problems.

Sadly, we didn't experience the unbridled joy that many families are filled with upon the arrival of a new baby. The happiness we did experience was accompanied by an omnipresent, on-the-edge feeling of knowing that at any moment something could go wrong and we'd lose Eric. My nerves were constantly frayed. Dealing with the myths surrounding my son's condition was also exhausting. When I took a trip to Mexico, one of my aunts suggested that I visit a well-known chapel of a virgin in a neighboring small town: "If you have faith, the *virgen* will cure your child." I told her that while I certainly *could* go with Eric, no amount of faith in a virgin would "cure" him. I patiently explained that even if he were somehow miraculously cured, it wouldn't be fair to the remaining hundreds of thousands of children with Down syndrome. I politely thanked my aunt for her good intentions and proceeded to explain to her what Down syndrome really was.

Prior to Eric's birth in October, I was expected to return to my position at the bank after the customary six weeks of maternity leave. Even though I expected that it would be more difficult after the baby, I also planned on completing my master's in business administration. Of course, this was my neat and logical thinking *before* Eric. The reality of my life *after* Eric was a completely different story.

Even though I was raised Catholic and attended catechism when I was young, I wondered what B.C. and A.D. meant. They were abbreviations I saw all the time but didn't think to ask about. Then I learned that they meant "before Christ" and *anno Domini,* "after Christ." That the entire world saw the birth of Christ as such a remarkable event that it divided history into two phases made sense to me.

A similar division occurred in how I began to understand my life's events. Eric was born and everything had changed; nothing in my life was recognizable. My life was split into what I had done before Eric came along and what my life would be like after he was born. It has been twenty-one years since Eric's birth—twenty-one years since I stopped planning my future. When people ask me what my next step is going to be, I usually shrug my shoulders and answer that I don't truly know. This is a strange response coming from someone who had previously developed a comprehensive life plan. All of my goals were attached to specific due dates. I had been taught to be thorough in my planning and that meant leaving no detail to chance. I would visualize, then execute. I had a five-, ten-, and twenty-year plan. I would climb the rungs of the bank ladder: vice president, senior vice president, and, eventually, president. I dreamed of becoming the chairwoman of my own financial institution. I even knew where I would travel for my well-deserved vacations—both before and after my early retirement at the age of sixty.

Eric's birth changed everything. I returned to work not six but eight weeks after my delivery. The bank's managers understood. I'll never forget Mr. Alex Kyman, the president of the bank, taking me aside. Of course I thought, *This is it. I'm done for. I'm losing my job, just what I needed.* Instead, he told me to simply try my best. He understood that I was going through a difficult time and the last thing I needed was to have to fear losing my job. "Whether you work an hour or forty hours a week, you'll have a guaranteed paycheck each week," he said. I was so relieved and grateful. The support he gave me was unparalleled. It's easy to see why he was one of the most successful bankers I have ever come across. He understood how to invest not only in finances, but also in his employees. He was a genuine leader and I'll always be indebted to him. I'll never forget the people who surrounded me during my darkest moments.

I continued to work as hard as I could at the bank. Sometimes that meant working twenty hours a week and sometimes it meant working forty. Unfortunately, Eric's health problems only worsened. At five months old, he started developing spasms. When these struck, his body would freeze as though startled and then contract for a second—and this same motion would repeat itself over and over. Eric's development was rapidly regressing. The pediatrician and neurologist's prognosis was bleak. The books we read said that infantile spasms often led to mental retardation. In cases like Eric's, where retardation already existed, profound mental retardation could develop. One day I called out Eric's name and he didn't even make an effort to search for my voice. His eyes floated around inside his head, not focusing on any one point. He looked distant, as though he was drifting further away with each passing day. He often stared at nothing with a blank expression. When we laid him down, he wouldn't fidget like other babies; his absolute stillness became eerie. I'd whisper in his ear that I loved him, but he wasn't able to turn his face to see me. I was desperate for help.

The medication he was taking made him extremely lethargic. He began to have sets of more than one hundred spasms throughout a day. We had to take him to the neurologist every week. It seemed as though nothing would work. So we gave him more medication—so much medication that it caused his pupils to ricochet inside their sockets like pinballs. And then one day his body stopped moving for longer than usual. Once again he was sped away to the emergency room. Eventually the crisis subsided, but the doctors told us, quite alarmingly, that they had never seen anything like this.

We continued to read everything we could about Down syndrome—something had to help and soon. My husband researched possible doctors who could help us, and when Eric was about nine months old, he came across a Dr. Mary Coleman. She was a pediatric neurologist in Washington, D.C., who had already seen fourteen children with both Down syndrome and infantile spasms (this, it turned out, was twice as many as the nearest ranking doctor in Texas). We called her office to ask if she'd be willing to see Eric.

She was initially hesitant because the distance between California and D.C. would not allow her to see Eric as often as she'd like. I insisted and then insisted some more. She sensed the desperation in my voice and finally acceded. She asked Eric's current neurologist to transfer his medical records. A few days later, we were welcomed into Dr. Coleman's home. She evaluated Eric and, for once, she told us we had reason to hope. This meant a lot coming from someone with her experience. She handed us a cortisol treatment and we administered it to him right then and there. In the time it took us to reach our hotel, we saw results. And, within twenty-four hours, Eric's spasms were cut in half. *This must be what it feels like to be blessed by a miracle,* I thought.

Dr. Coleman restored our faith in Eric. However, she put an onus on us: "You're going to get out of Eric as much as you put into him." She explained that the more we worked with Eric, the greater his chances of recovering the ground he had lost in his development. She informed us that even though he was technically a nine-month-old, for all intents and purposes, he might as well have been born that very day in her office. Eric was going to require (at least) double the amount of early intervention to regain everything he had lost with the spasms. That meant a whole array of therapy: physical, occupational, speech, and others.

On our flight back to Los Angeles, my husband and I discussed how we would manage Eric's care. We had been given another chance to care for Eric and didn't want to risk the slightest error. We threw around a few scenarios, but I already knew what needed to be done.

Stepping Off the Ladder

I knew I just had to do it. I needed to gather the courage to walk into Mr. Kyman's office and resign from my position at the bank. Eric needed me full-time. As understanding and generous as the bank had been—they had even offered to pay for my trip to D.C.—I would've felt as though I was abusing their kindness if I continued to work there. Also, although I hadn't planned to, I had become pregnant again. I told Mr. Kyman all of this.

He let out a long sigh. "I understand your decision, Rosario, but if you ever decide to come back, just say the word and we'll find something for you."

I was speechless. This man had once again shown his compassion. I gave him a hug and, with my shoulders slouched forward, pushed open his office door. At that moment, I fully understood the expression "to have a heavy heart."

Settling In

That first week was rough as I tried to get accustomed to my new lifestyle. I was used to running back and forth between Eric and the bank, never away too long, but having moments, however small, to myself. I tried as best I could to fulfill my position as Eric's full-time mother. He was only five months old when I became pregnant for the second time. Although I knew it would be even more work, I was excited about the limitless possibilities for this new baby. Whether or not Alex and I acknowledged it, I think we both felt that somehow this new baby would grant us all of the wonderfully typical first-time parent experiences that we had missed out on.

With a new mother's zeal, I bought a whole closet's worth of new maternity clothes. This child would signal a new beginning for us. I didn't even care about the gender of this baby; the only thing that mattered was that it was healthy. I began to dream again. When people found out that I was pregnant some were obviously happy for me, but others showed concern. I was asked if I'd considered an amniocentesis (a procedure to help diagnosis fetal abnormalities). I rejected this possibility because of the associated risks. The testing was invasive and could lead to a miscarriage. I wasn't willing to take a chance like that with my new baby. Besides, I knew that this would be the perfect child. And, in the off chance that there was a problem, I already had the confidence to deal with a child that had disabilities. I had learned how to navigate an often circuitous health-care system. Even if the tests revealed a child with any sort of defect, what could I do about it? I would never consider abortion an option for me. Of course, it's such an individual decision, but I knew that I'd never be able to go through with it. I had no doubt that this baby was going to be the best gift God could possibly give me. That is, of course, if God happened to be in the giving mood.

4. Spiraling Downward

I eagerly awaited my sonogram. I knew in an abstract sort of way there was a precious baby growing inside me, but something about a sonogram makes a pregnancy a more concrete reality. Not too long ago, I had been looking at my little Eric on a similar monitor.

The technician asked me to lie down. I hopped onto the table and made myself as comfortable as my four-months-pregnant belly allowed. The technician busied herself with untangling cords and setting up the equipment. She finally squared herself with the monitor. In a few moments, I'd have a glimpse into my womb where I imagined my baby nestled warmly. I couldn't wait to see him or her, and I began to bombard the technician with questions.

"What is it? A he or she? Can you already tell? How big is it? Can you make out any of its features?"

"It'll just take a minute." She chuckled. "Sometimes it takes a while for the image to come through."

"Oh, okay, how about now?" I asked a minute later.

"There's nothing like an expecting mother's glow." She smiled.

We made small talk while she continued to knowingly turn knobs and stare down the machine. A few more minutes passed. She nodded to what I was saying, but her face was now contorted in frustration. She turned the monitor away from me and leaned into it. She wore a blank expression.

"Can I please see the monitor?" I asked. "I want to see my baby."

"Miss, you're going to have to talk to the doctor."

"Well, with my first baby's sonogram, the technician let me see the monitor," I said, "and she even gave me a picture to take home as a souvenir."

"Miss, I'm sorry, but you're just going to have to wait to see the doctor."

"Is there something wrong?" The question tripped out of my mouth.

"Like I said, I'm not at liberty—"

"Just tell me what's wrong," I interrupted. "I don't need to hear it from a doctor."

"Please tell the front desk when you'll be available tomorrow to come in," she said. The tail of her lab coat trailed behind her like a billowing cape as she exited the room. I attempted to stand, but my legs jerked around awkwardly as though they belonged to a marionette.

Moments later I was home. Someone must've tugged my strings, guiding me home safely, because I was in front of my door with no recollection of how I got there.

The phone rang, shattering the numbing daze I was in. It was Kaiser. "Yes, I'll come in tomorrow. Yes, I'm fine. I don't care if my regular doctor isn't in. Anybody will do."

I placed the phone on its receiver and without removing

my hand, I lifted it back up to call Alex at work. I tried not to worry him, but something in my voice must have betrayed me because he said he was on his way home.

Alex arrived and I collapsed into his arms as though someone had cut my strings. I cried while he held me up. We talked for hours and braced ourselves for the worst while hoping for the best. It was a night filled with tossing, turning, and no sleep. Occasionally, Alex would gently nudge me.

"Are you awake?" he'd ask.

"Of course. You?"

"Well, I just asked you. So, yes."

On and on it went in cycles throughout the night. Alex nudged me and I nudged him. Restless from mind laps, I turned onto my side and placed my hand on my belly, whispering, "I love you." I muffled my sobs in my pillow. I hoped for a miracle. I'd wake up and everything would be okay, just fine. The last thing I remember before I drifted off to sleep were the dawn's birds chirping outside my window.

"Well, you must suspect that something isn't right," said the doctor that morning, obviously intent on diving right in.

"I guess," I said, gripping my husband's hand.

The doctor took a deep breath and lowered his glasses to the tip of his nose.

"Your baby is no more," he said. "There was no heartbeat yesterday and that's why the technician couldn't give you details."

Down, down, down I went. I was drowning, gasping for air; my head was spinning. I thought I'd pass out. The change in my pocket jingled from my body's shaking. In that instant, all my hopes and dreams for my baby and our family vanished.

"So would you rather have a dilation and curettage right now, or have nature take its course with a miscarriage?" he asked, not missing a beat.

The doctor's voice was garbled as though I were under water. His lips moved, but I had no idea what he was saying. He turned to Alex and repeated the question. My husband just shook his head back and forth, not giving the doctor an answer. After a long pause, I surfaced, gasping for air, and I asked the doctor for his professional opinion.

"I suggest you let nature take its course and when you begin to feel contractions come to the emergency room," he said. "We'll give nature up to two weeks. Of course, we'll have to study the fetus."

The heartache when we left the hospital was a true physical pain. My husband and I locked hands during the entire trip back home. We saw no point in talking. No words could approximate the turmoil both of us were feeling or take the pain away. I rubbed my chest. The pervading silence was in stark contrast to the voice in my head that screamed rhetorical questions: *Why so much punishment? Why me? What could I have done to prevent it? Why can't I have this baby? Why is my womb so toxic for a baby? Don't I deserve some happiness?*

I was in a state of denial. I hoped for a miracle. Maybe the doctor was wrong. Maybe the technician didn't know what she was doing. I told myself anything to keep my baby-in-the-womb illusion from bursting. At its worst this meant having one-sided conversations while rubbing my belly. In my heart,

I knew even then that I was fooling myself, that I'd have to accept the harsh reality: I was carrying a dead baby.

I followed the doctor's instructions, but with each passing day it was getting harder to look at myself in the mirror. My protruding belly was a constant reminder of loss. There was no more laughter. There was no more hope. There was no more anything. I couldn't imagine how I'd ever be able to smile or laugh again. I cradled a dead baby inside my womb for exactly two weeks before nature ran its course and I began to have contractions.

When we arrived at the emergency room, the hospital staff was ready for us. The contractions had grown more painful on the drive to the hospital. I was reaching my threshold for pain on all levels. This pain, this physical pain, was all for nothing and I wanted nothing to do with this procedure. My regular obstetrician Dr. Cesar Caldera happened to be on call for the emergency room. He'd always been so kind, gentle, and thoughtful with me. He knew my entire history with Eric and had taken care of me in the initial stages of this pregnancy. He hovered over my bed. I cried in agony and begged him to take the pain away.

"I'll remove the fetus, Rosario, but your true pain is another story." He gripped my hand for a few seconds and then injected me with something. I immediately passed out.

When I came to several hours later, I was in the same sterile hospital room. So it was true. It had not been just some bad dream. My husband was to my right. When I looked at the sorrowful expression on his face I began to weep. I ran my hand over my deflated belly. It was over. No more pain. No more baby. No more hope.

The following weekend I returned my maternity wardrobe, tags still hooked into their collars.

"Are you exchanging these already?" The sales associate was the same lady who had helped me only a few weeks before.

"No, I'll no longer need these," I said, taking the clothes out of the plastic bag and swinging them onto the counter.

"Excuse me?"

"I lost my baby." Each time I said it out loud, I had to confront the harsh reality.

"Oh, I am *so* sorry." She came around to the other side of the counter and gave me a hug. I melted in her embrace.

How Low Could I Go?

A couple of weeks later the test results from examining the fetus were in. It would've been a baby girl who would've been born with Turner's syndrome—a rare chromosomal disorder in females characterized by short stature and the lack of sexual development at puberty. Unlike Down syndrome where there's an extra chromosome, Turner's syndrome is a result of missing all (or a part) of an X chromosome. The geneticist said that the chances of having a baby with Down syndrome followed by one with Turner's syndrome was "one in a million." This meant nothing to me. As I saw it, if I were *the* one in the million, then it might as well have been a 100 percent chance. The doctor asked if we had thought of conceiving again. My husband and I looked at each other with blank expressions; no words were necessary. I couldn't even fathom the thought. My husband told her it would be a long time. I agreed, a long time . . . as in never again!

Losing my baby girl was the metaphorical straw that broke the camel's back. I was slipping down a slick spiral slide, with nothing to stop my accelerating descent. I took stock of my life in the past year: a child with Down syndrome and a slew of other medical problems; a position at a bank that I had to leave; a dream of getting my M.B.A. shattered; a beautiful house sold because we couldn't afford the mortgage; and the latest, a miscarriage that happened to reveal a fetus with Turner's syndrome. It was official: my life had fallen apart. I could throw my hands up now. Long gone were the days when I felt I could do it all. The sky was once the limit, and now it was coming down on me and fast. I felt like I was being pelted by disaster after disaster. I had no control. I was hopeless. I became desolate. Many mornings, I didn't even step out of my pajamas. Showering also became optional. The only constant in my life was taking care of Eric. I became a mechanical version of my previous self, the gears inside me revolved to feed, change, and bathe Eric.

On the occasions when I did manage to "snap out of it," what I saw filled me with resentment toward everyone, especially toward the person I saw the most often: my husband Alex. One of the many aspects of our relationship that had always united us was a shared desire to succeed. During the first four years of marriage, we both worked full-time jobs and attended night classes. Most Saturday and Sunday nights were spent on "dates" at the library. We were both immigrants (he was from Nicaragua) and we were set on achieving the American Dream even if we never articulated it as such. We kept each other going, we quizzed each other, woke each other up when one of us accidentally fell asleep with our nose in a book. We had always balanced each other. He was reserved and I was outgoing. He was objective and I was emotional. We both regarded marriage and family as the most important pillars in our life. So why was *I* the one making all the sacrifices, while *he* continued to work at his I.T. job for the city of Los Angeles and take his M.B.A. classes? Even when he came home exhausted after a long day of work and school, I imagined a smirk on his face. All he wanted was to hug and kiss his child and wife. All I wanted was to punch him in the nose.

I was plagued by the worst headaches and rarely ate. I used to love going to the movies, and a little retail therapy always seemed to do the trick in the past. Not now. My husband worried about me. He gently suggested I consider getting help. I told him that I didn't need help. If he had a problem, he could seek help. What was the point of getting help when nothing could change what had happened? No one could make all this right. I couldn't take it anymore. I couldn't go on. I was too tired. I was bitter and resentful. I was not the happy person I used to be. When I went to sleep, I'd pray that I wouldn't wake up—that God would take pity on me and relinquish me from these "mortal coils." And yet, morning after morning my eyes would open, allowing the desperation to flood back in. I constantly felt like screaming; unfortunately, that required energy I did not have.

I began to drop weight as effortlessly as a cat sheds fur. My skin color changed to an unhealthy hue. I was beyond despondent. One day my husband held me tightly. He no longer suggested I see someone; he insisted. I reluctantly agreed. I went to a regular medical doctor and within a few minutes rattled off the last year's events. When I was done, he cleared his throat and spoke with a trepidation usually reserved for talking people off ledges.

"Wow, you've certainly had a rough time lately. Listen, I'm not going to give you any prescriptions. Instead, I want you to do me the favor of staying near your phone. Later today, a doctor friend of mine will contact you. I want you to explain exactly what you just told me. He'll be able to evaluate you and decide on the best course of action. How does that sound to you?"

I shrugged my shoulders. In retrospect, I'm certain that he was concerned. Although the word *suicide* was never uttered, I'm sure he thought I was a likely candidate. His doctor friend called me right way. He must've ruled out suicide after our conversation because my appointment to see a psychologist was set for a few days later. I had never seriously considered suicide, although I began to understand how many do. I only wished that I'd never wake up—it was more passive than suicide. Either way, I was probably at the phase right before people actively start contemplating suicide.

A couple of days later, I found myself facing a psychologist for the first time in my life. He had a kind, gentle, unhurried demeanor. I recapped the past year of my life. I explained how only a year ago I was on top of the world; my life was *almost* perfect. The only thing missing was a baby. I had seen myself as a young, sassy professional looking forward to a big promotion at the bank. I was on my way to getting my M.B.A. I was married to a wonderful man with whom I owned a beautiful home. I had even done some traveling to Europe. By all accounts, we had made it. The only thing missing was that long-awaited baby. Yes, the baby came, but he had Down syndrome and with that, all I had worked for was gone. Eric had had so many medical problems that I had to quit my career, give up my M.B.A., and sell my house—not to mention almost losing Eric twice and then, most recently, the miscarriage. I just couldn't take it anymore. I wanted to be put out of my suffering.

He listened to me attentively and asked a lot of questions. I was boiling over with emotions: anger, sadness, helplessness, hopelessness, and resentment. None of these feelings were exactly life affirming. And although I had not faced it, I felt a sense of resentment toward the expectations that were placed on me by my family, culture, and religion. The values I had been raised with required that I accept everything and smile. My own mother said she understood, but I snapped back, "You never had to raise a child who is mentally retarded." As I heard myself articulating feelings and thoughts that I had failed to acknowledge, I was overcome by a feeling of anger that washed over me, annihilating all other convoluted feelings. I was experiencing a clarity that I hadn't felt in months.

It didn't make sense for me to give up my professional life, my education, my home, and lose a child and simply stand by without complaint. Deep inside of me, I was rebelling against all the beliefs I had up until that point held so dearly. As a mother, I was supposed to sacrifice anything for my children, including life itself. I was not supposed to grumble, but instead count my blessings. What kind of a mother would leave her "sick" child to go to work? As a wife, I shouldn't even consider bringing up that option with my husband—even if he was making less money and I had greater potential for advancement with the bank. Everyone in my family—especially the most religious ones—made sure to remind me that all these hardships were really "blessings in disguise." Every time someone said something like that to me, I'd ask God to please go bless someone else; I'd rather take my blessings without disguises, thank you very much. Other times, when I couldn't help but be sarcastic, I'd tell people that I hoped God would bless them in the same way I'd been blessed. I'd ask if they perhaps needed some of my "blessings" because as far as I was concerned, I had more than my lifetime supply. I know I must have sounded disrespectful to my family and other well-intentioned people; I felt they had no moral authority to say such euphemistic and empty things when they had not gone through the same experiences I had been through.

After a long session (the room was now bathed in an orange glow from the streetlights), the psychologist turned to me with fingers in a downward steeple position. He delivered his assessment with a warm voice: "Well, I can see why you're feeling the way you are. Many people face difficulties out of their own doing, but your case is very different. You've had no control over the things that have happened to you, but simply stated, you still have choices to make."

"What? Are you kidding me? What's my choice?" I was stunned. It couldn't be that simple.

"If you want to go back to work, you can do that tomorrow. If that's really what you want to do, then you can do that. But, if you want to stay home and take care of your son, well, that's your choice, too."

"What are you talking about? What about everybody?" I said. My whole family trampled on my shoulders.

"It doesn't matter what everyone else says or thinks," he continued, making sure to make eye contact with me. "It is *your* life and as such, it's *your* choice," he added with finality.

"You mean I can choose to stay at home, too?"

"Yes, it's your choice!"

The shackles of resentment slipped onto the floor. It all began to make sense. I was empowered for the first time in months. I didn't have to blame anybody because (with great clarity) I saw that staying home with Eric was a choice I had made, albeit passively. Now, if I wanted to, I could start making active decisions. It made a world of difference to me to see that despite the perceived pressures placed on me by my family, culture, and religion, I was still free to choose what I wanted. Whatever people expected of me was not important. What truly mattered was my reaction to what was happening to me. There were plenty of people who were trained to take care of babies with disabilities. I wasn't going to be the first or last mother to enlist someone's help to take care of my baby. But if I wanted to stay home and take care of Eric, I was free to do that, too. It truly was up to me. This was so simple, yet it was a profound revelation to me at the time.

The psychologist suggested I come back to see him in a week. I thanked him profusely for helping me see what I had failed to acknowledge all along, but I told him I most likely wouldn't return. And I never did see him again. To this day, even though I can't remember the name of the psychologist, I am grateful to him. His simple declaration—"It's your choice"—were three powerful words that have helped me time and time again.

In my car, on the way back home from the psychologist's office, I took a deep breath and made the conscious decision to stay home and take care of Eric. If I ever wanted to return to work, it would be there waiting. Having options made me feel lighter. Almost magically, the resentment I had been holding against my husband and family dissipated.

5. A Family Is Born

No more babies! Who would want more children after the experiences I had had? One child born with Down syndrome and the other miscarried and diagnosed with Turner's syndrome? In my book, two "complicated" pregnancies in a row was not promising. Besides, Eric needed my undivided attention. Dr. Coleman—the doctor we met with in D.C.—had told us that Eric could recover from all developmental losses he had experienced, but it was largely up to us to make sure he progressed. She reminded us that the more work we put in to his development, the more we'd see results.

Raised Catholic, I was taught never to use the contraceptive pill because it was unnatural. Catholicism, like several other religions, sees the body as a temple not to be desecrated with drinking, smoking, drugs, and other substances that alter the body's chemistry. Before getting married, I attended a church-sponsored class that taught natural fertility regulation using the Billings Ovulation Method. Unfortunately, this method was not as effective as we needed it to be, and Alex and I decided that I'd start to take the pill. A couple of years went by and then my body began to have an adverse reaction to it. I gained weight and had terrible mood swings. With no good reason, I'd jump down everyone's throats. During a checkup, I told a doctor that I didn't have any friends. My husband began to tiptoe around me, worried that something he did would set me off. The doctor suggested I stop taking the pill. I was frightened of getting pregnant again, but I knew that if I continued to take the pill it would only get worse.

To avoid another pregnancy, we began to follow the Billings method again; we made sure to keep diligent track of my body's temperature, charting it on a graph, and abstained from sex whenever there was a higher risk of pregnancy. But, it didn't work. Soon after going off of the pill, I became pregnant again. The doctor explained that sometimes when a woman has been on the pill for a while, it takes time for her hormones to return to the way they used to operate. This explained why the rhythm method had failed us. Here we were again. Another pregnancy. I was distressed. What if there were problems again? What if he or she had a disability? What if I miscarried again? It was absolute torture. We decided not to tell anyone about my pregnancy, and that included my mom. I didn't want her to be consumed with worry. Besides, this was a personal matter, and we didn't want anyone's opinion to influence our actions. Based on my doctor's advice, we decided to have a chorionic villi sampling (CVS). This was a somewhat new test in 1985 and carried a higher risk of miscarriage than amniocentesis; it's performed earlier in the pregnancy (usually at ten weeks) and the preliminary results are given within twenty-four hours—as opposed to an amniocentesis, which is performed at sixteen weeks with the results in two weeks.

My doctor carefully reviewed my medical history and suggested I take the CVS test. Kaiser performed this procedure for only a select group of at-risk mothers. As the day of the test approached, I was a nervous wreck. This knotted nervousness was becoming an all-too-familiar feeling. I tried to distract myself, but it was no use. I knew I couldn't take another hit. I begged God to spare me. I deserved to experience the unfettered joy of motherhood that had eluded me. My husband Alex's palm was sealed to mine with sweat. I was told that the procedure wouldn't take long; the doctor would suction some of the villi surrounding my placenta and then culture those cells. After he was done with the procedure, the doctor gave me specific instructions to go home and rest. We didn't want to risk having a miscarriage. Alex carried me, like a child, to our bedroom upstairs. As I lay on my back and stared up at the ceiling, my tears began to pour. The waiting game began yet again: another twenty-four hours of sleeplessness.

What if the test came back with more disappointment? What if this baby also had Down syndrome, Turner's syndrome, or some other syndrome I'd soon have to become an expert on? Would we tell everyone immediately or wait until the baby was born? What if I had another miscarriage? I was consumed with fear and prayed silently, then loudly. The words I uttered were coated with optimism, confidence, and absolute fear. But mostly I had no idea what I was feeling. I thought through various scenarios and developed contingency plans. I knew that even if this baby had a disability, Alex and I would never truly consider an abortion. We'd be riddled with guilt because it went against all of our religious, familial, and cultural values. So if an abortion was out of the question, what would we do? Clarity was out of reach because these questions did not have answers. I caressed my tummy while whispering to my baby. Even if this pregnancy had come unexpectedly, it was certainly wanted. I asked God to spare this child any disability. I prayed to the Virgen de Guadalupe, hoping that as a mother she'd understand my plight.

By midmorning the phone rang. I let it ring again, again, and one last time before I finally picked it up. The receptionist from the doctor's office asked that I hold while she transferred me to the doctor. I held my breath.

"Well, the test results are in and you'll be glad to know everything's okay," he said.

"Okay?" I said.

"Yes, you're having a baby girl," he said.

I was speechless.

"Hello, are you there, Mrs. Marín?"

"Yes, yes I'm here, thank you so much," I finally said as I recovered. With the dropping of the phone receiver into its cradle, the weight dropped from my shoulders.

Tears fell again, but this time to express an indescribable happiness. Eric would have a sister and her name would be Carmen, after my mother. We had agreed on her name long ago when my brother and sister were expecting their babies. As my mom's first daughter, I felt entitled to name my daughter after the wonderful woman who had taught me so much. Thankfully, no one had chosen Carmen as a name for their daughters—even though she would be the fifth granddaughter. My brothers and sisters were kind in honoring my request. Carmen means "song," and I certainly felt like singing that day; she'd be the song that would fill my heart. I couldn't thank God and the Virgen de Guadalupe enough.

It would be months before any remaining fears faded and were replaced by the anticipation of having Carmen in my arms. I was dreaming again of my family's future: Eric and Carmen playing, my husband teaching her to read. I imagined her Quinceañera, wedding, and future children. There was no way I was going to take any chances with this delivery. I asked the doctor to schedule a C-section. I had already had one with Eric and knew it would mean less risk for Carmen. The doctor agreed.

The day of the delivery arrived. We left for the hospital at six A.M. and I had the C-section at eight A.M. My husband was in the delivery room with me. When Carmen was finally shown to us and was indeed a baby girl, it still felt like a surprise. She was the most beautiful baby girl I had ever seen; her skin was the most delicate brown, as if she had been given a perfect tan; her eyes were big and black. When she smiled, the most adorable dimple in her right cheek revealed itself. Quite simply, she was perfect.

God had answered my prayers. Eric had a healthy baby sister and it felt like a complete family. I'll never be able to fully express what a blessing Carmen has been in our family from the day of her birth onward.

Death Comes Knocking . . . Again

When I was five months pregnant with Carmen, Eric had a major neck operation to fix his Atlantoaxial Instability—

because he was becoming paralyzed. After the operation, he was required to wear halo bracing for six months to ensure that his neck wouldn't move. It was difficult to see my child with four (approximately three-inch) screws going into his head. After the six months passed, the neurosurgeon thought it best to keep the apparatus fastened to Eric until after Carmen was born. Eric was almost four years old and becoming skilled at zooming around the house in his customized walker and halo. Time and time again, Eric's adaptability would astound me: he was a true fighter.

How much he'd have to fight became clear when Carmen was only five weeks old. While I breast-fed Carmen, my best friend Locha and I were chatting in the living room. Locha was commenting on how wonderful it was that Eric could get around on his walker. We both looked over at him as he planted his two feet up against the television screen. I yanked Carmen from my breast and handed her to Locha. Before I could make it to Eric, he had kicked himself away from the television with a force that threw him off balance. He thumped onto his back. The cry that erupted from him was unlike anything I had ever heard—it was deafening. Three of the four screws from the halo were no longer attached to his head and the fourth had pierced the back of his skull.

Time slowed, much like dramatic moments in movies. My eyes couldn't believe what they were seeing. I was mere moments from passing out when my husband came rushing down the stairs. I officially lost it and kept on repeating: "Alex, he's going to die! Eric is going to die!" My husband was visibly panicked. He shouted for me to shut up and control myself. The whole experience was a blur. I don't remember who called the paramedics. Despite my best efforts, all I could do was continue to yell and scream. I was no help. When the paramedics arrived, I remember one of them said that he'd never seen anything like it. "Well, does anybody have any great ideas?" he added. I was dizzy.

Next thing I knew, I was inside a wailing ambulance slicing through traffic, shifting cars onto the sides of the road as though parting water. I was seated in the front with the driver and the paramedics were in the back with Eric. My poor son looked conscious, but confused and in a great amount of pain. I must've been so panicked that I came emotionally full circle and was soon overtaken by a feeling of absolute peace. I had a flashback to when I was nineteen and attended a weekend retreat called Encuentros. The events of the weekend culminated in participants placing their right hands on the Bible and declaring their faith in God. It was a powerful religious experience for me because I felt like I was communicating directly with God.

In my absolute desperation, the feeling of that moment rushed back with soothing clarity. I prayed with all the religious fervor that had originally been awakened in me on that retreat. I have no idea whether I was praying in my own head or out loud. I told God that I believed in him now more than ever. I told him that after everything I had been through with Eric, I hoped it was his will that Eric should live. Instantly, an indescribable peacefulness pervaded through me. I felt serene.

I was lucid when we arrived in the hospital's emergency room, providing all necessary information to the admissions clerk. My husband made sure that Carmen was taken care of and arrived in a frantic state a few minutes later. I must have appeared to be in a daze. He started to ask a flurry of questions.

"Try to calm down, Alex. Everything is going to be just fine." I touched his shoulder as though I could transfer my tranquility. He must have thought I had lost it, considering only moments ago I had been screaming at the top of my lungs.

"Sure, Rosario, I'll calm down while our son is in there with a screw pierced right through his skull!"

"I know how it looks, but trust me, Eric will pull through this one."

Once they stabilized Eric, the neurosurgeon ordered an ambulance to transfer him to another hospital in Anaheim. It was five A.M. The neurosurgeon spoke frankly about what he planned to do and its possible consequences. He presented us with the worst-case scenario: Eric could die. They'd try their best to remove the pin without causing any damage, but there could still be serious complications. I imagined the neurosurgeon removing the lacerating pin and brain matter spilling out through the punctured hole.

Thank God nothing as dramatic as that happened. The doctor removed the halo and Eric was immediately placed in the intensive care unit. The neurosurgeon showed us the disturbing X-rays and told us that he feared the consequence of an infection to the brain lining. I continued to repeat: "Eric will be fine." Everyone thought I was in denial.

Throughout most of this week-long ordeal, I had my six-week-old Carmen at my side, even though babies were not allowed in the hospital. I whispered in her ear that she had to be very quiet so that she could stay with us. If the hospital staff knew she was with me, they'd make me take her home. I didn't want to leave her with anyone; she was giving me strength. The first three days Eric was in intensive care and, since only one person could be at his side at a time, my husband and I took turns cradling Carmen in the adjoining family room. Once Eric's condition improved, he was moved out of the ICU and into another room. Seeing as how Carmen had yet to be discovered, we continued to bring her with us. Since a family member was with Eric at every moment, the nurses would call on that person if anything happened. Eric was checked at the same times every day so we were able to anticipate when we'd have to hide Carmen. We alternated between taking her out of the room or into the bathroom. Luckily she spent most of her time silently sleeping during those first few weeks of her life.

In the end, the doctors couldn't believe that Eric had been spared any complications. The day we left the hospital, the nurses were surprised to find out that Carmen had been there with me the entire time. It seemed as if Carmen was knowingly deferring to her brother's needs. At a time when most babies require so much attention, my baby girl seemed understanding of the situation. We were mystified.

This would be the first of many times that Carmen would grace the entire family with her sensitivity and innate understanding of her brother's needs. Carmen quickly became my constant companion, right alongside me as I took care of her brother. When Carmen was about five years old, I asked if she wouldn't mind coming with me to a friend's funeral. My friend had died of cancer and I was asked to give her eulogy.

Driving back home, I took Carmen's little hand and thanked her for being with me on this sad day. I knew it was late and way past her bedtime. She took a moment, as though absorbing what I had said, and then spoke words that I'll never forget: "But Mom, that's why I was born . . . to be your partner." How was it possible for this little girl to understand how much I needed her?

A couple of years later, as I was tucking Carmen into bed, I lay down next to her and told her that sometimes I felt remorseful about not being able to spend as much time as I wanted with her. Again she took a moment, and then, looking up at me with those black sparkling eyes, she smiled and said, "That's okay, Mommy, you're helping other people." Once again, she amazed me with her incredible empathy.

Not Again!

My husband wanted another child. More specifically, he wanted another boy. He loved Eric very much and thought it would be good for his development to have a brother. Carmen was over a year old at this point and had brought many cherished moments into our life. We had the best family one could ever hope for; why risk another pregnancy? I was hesitant, to say the least. Pregnancy for me had always entailed navigating through a turbulent sea of emotions.

I hoped that my husband would, in time, drop the whole idea. No such luck. He persisted even though he knew there was a 50 percent chance that we'd have another girl. He wanted to take that chance. In my husband's face I saw how much having another child meant to him. In retrospect, we were perhaps feeling more confident after Carmen's successful birth. Alex felt strongly that another baby boy was in the cards. I finally caved in and said yes. We agreed not to tell anyone about our desire to have another baby. It was difficult enough to go through all the turmoil without the familial audience standing by. We decided that until we knew the result of the CVS exam (the same exam we had had with Carmen) we wouldn't tell anyone.

My mind and body began to process the all-too-familiar emotions that came with pregnancy. I was more confident than I had ever been with any of my three previous pregnancies. I already knew how to take care of a child with a disability and no longer saw it as an earth-shattering event. If it turned out to be a girl, I knew that she would be welcomed into our loving family. I tried to remain blind to the possibly dark outcomes. The only immediate fear was losing my baby due to the CVS testing. I waited patiently next to the phone for the results.

When I got the call from the doctor's office the next day, I braced myself for the worst but hoped for the best. Then came the three words I had been hoping for: "Everything looks fine." I crossed my fingers and asked if it was a boy or a girl. The doctor informed me that I was having a boy. I screamed. "I take it that you are happy about that," the doctor said, chuckling. I couldn't wait for my husband to come home and called his work number to give him the news. He was ecstatic and insisted that we go out that night to celebrate. We had already decided that we would name the baby Alex after my husband. Although technically my husband's first name is Alvaro and his middle name is Alejandro, everyone simply calls him Alex. It was as though he would be the junior.

My pregnancy was a happy one and we waited for Baby Alex's arrival with great anticipation. My life had grown hectic with volunteering, traveling to advocate for people with disabilities, and, most importantly, raising my two children. As I had done during Carmen's pregnancy, I told the doctor I wanted to have a C-section; this would minimize any risk to the baby. Having already had two C-sections, I was well acquainted with the potential risks to myself and was willing to go through it one more time. Without a doubt, this was going to be my last pregnancy. My husband and I had already agreed that they would tie my tubes during the C-section. If for some reason I ended up delivering the baby naturally, then Alex would have a vasectomy.

The doctor agreed to the operation and we set the delivery date. But if life had taught me anything, it was that plans don't always—if rarely—proceed as anticipated. Six weeks before the due date, I experienced what felt like contractions. We rushed to the hospital. I was a nervous wreck because if these were indeed contractions, that meant I was having a premature baby. When we arrived at the emergency room, they checked for any signs of problems. They gave me medication to stop what were indeed contractions. Within a few hours, they were able to release me. It was a close call but if everything went according to plan, I would deliver a full-term baby.

I visited my mom a couple of days later. She had always been so nurturing to all the pregnant women in the family. She made me cantaloupe melon water (my favorite drink) and it was refreshing. At around one P.M., I felt an incredible urgency to go to the bathroom. I didn't make it there before my water broke. "The baby is on the way!" I screamed, running back to the kitchen. I was rushed to the emergency room—yet again—and was filled with both excitement and fear.

When we arrived at the hospital, the doctor and his attendees were preparing for the operation. The doctor began to run through his checks and then asked me if I had consumed anything recently. "Just some cantaloupe water," I told him. He explained that they would have to wait another six hours before they could attempt the C-section. The contractions were coming regularly, but I took comfort in knowing that they would at least stop at seven P.M. They plugged me in to monitoring equipment. I asked for something to help me with the pain, but they said they couldn't give me anything because of the impending surgery.

My family knew that the surgery wouldn't come for a few more hours, so I was alone with my husband in the room. When a contraction flooded over me, I'd remind myself that this was natural—the baby was trying to make his way into the world. I patted my belly, saying, "Soon, my little Alex, soon." At five-thirty P.M. I felt another undeniable urge to go to the bathroom and called out for the nurse to remove all of the monitoring equipment. She came in and as soon as she gave me the once over, panic plastered her face.

"Oh my God, the baby is here! Don't move!" she said, exiting the room. Seconds later the doctor came rushing in.

"Don't push, whatever you do, don't push. We have to get you to the delivery room," the doctor said.

There was no time for the C-section. It all happened so fast. In a matter of moments, I was holding a baby boy in my arms. I was in shock. I just kept repeating: "I don't believe it! I don't believe it! The baby is already here!" He was precious, tiny, beautiful, and impatient. My husband had been with me through the entire delivery and had the tears of a proud father coating his eyes. He certainly wasn't thinking of the vasectomy he would now need to have.

Because Alex was a premature baby, he'd have to stay in the hospital for monitoring. I pleaded with the doctors to allow me to take the baby home when I was released the next day. The doctor said that he'd assess the baby's progress and let us know his decision. I knew my baby would thrive in a loving home environment. The next morning, the doctor said that Alex had done very well overnight. He would allow me to take him home since I had taken CPR classes and had experience dealing with children that demanded lots of attention. The one caveat was that I had to promise to bring Alex in every single day for a week and thereafter as they saw fit. Of course I agreed to these terms.

Our homecoming was overwhelmingly joyous. Cradling Alex and surrounded by my two other children and husband, I knew our complete family had been born. I was blessed and couldn't ask for anything more. Alex quickly became an integral part of the family. His nickname became *gusanito,* little worm, because even when there was a small space between me and anyone or anything, he'd wiggle his way onto my lap. He was always so eager to see me, kicking his feet in anticipation when I was near.

As he grew older, he continued to be very attached to me. He was such a content and happy child, always ready to offer a hug or kiss. He believes I am the best chef in the world. Anything I cook, he enjoys. One day he asked me how my food could taste so delicious. I told him that when I cook, I sprinkle *piscas de amor*—dashes of love. To this day, he still asks me to not forget the *piscas* in my cooking.

I have taken great satisfaction in seeing the relationships develop among my three children. Although Eric is the oldest (now twenty-one years old), Carmen and Alex are both protective of him. When Alex was six years old, the entire family sat down to watch a television special about what families need to do before, during, and after a fire. After the show, we developed a plan of action and agreed on a meeting location. The three bedrooms were located on the second floor with a long hallway separating the master bedroom from the children's rooms. We discussed how in the event of a fire, we'd all have to jump out of our respective windows if the hallway and the stairs caught on fire. Since Alex and Eric shared a room, I let Alex know that Eric most likely would probably be too frightened to jump out of their bedroom window. "If that's the case, you still need to jump out the window yourself," I said. Alex nodded his head okay, but he seemed troubled by the idea.

A couple of hours later, Alex nudged me.

"I've been thinking about the fire, Mommy."

"What were you thinking?" I asked.

"If Eric doesn't jump out the window, I won't either. I'll stay and die with him."

My heart cringed. That Alex had the maturity to not want his brother to die alone is something I'll never forget.

"It makes me so happy to see how much you love your brother," I said, hugging him tightly. "How about we come up with a better solution?"

"Like what?" he asked.

"Well, how about you push Eric out the window before you jump?"

"Yes. That'll work," he said, content that we had found a better solution.

Alex has always had a big heart, and today, at fifteen years old, he has grown to be a noble young man. I still cherish the moments when unbeknownst to him I catch the slightest gesture or snippet of conversation that demonstrates how gentle and protective he is of Eric. Alex—the once tiny premature baby—has grown to be six feet tall, whereas Eric is almost five feet tall. My heart still soars every time I see them side-by-side. Eric's influence on Alex's life is clear: he takes strong exception when his teenager friends playfully call each other "retard." He makes it known that he doesn't think it's funny and his friends have had to apologize for being insensitive.

Eric's influence in my life was also clear, but that it would completely alter the landscape of my future was something I hadn't anticipated.

6. Living with Purpose

After the initial denial that Eric's Down syndrome wasn't something that would go away or improve remarkably despite our greatest efforts, I arrived at a peaceful place of acceptance. At first, I had trouble wrapping my mind around the fact that the life I had initially planned out and envisioned would never materialize. My son—through no fault of his own—would never be able to do all the things I had imagined for him. As painful as it was, this was my new reality that suggested many unexplored dimensions. If I was to become the best mother I could be for Eric, I had to figure out how he fit into my life. I needed to become an expert on Down syndrome—a condition I knew little about until Eric's birth.

There are many myths surrounding Down syndrome and, unfortunately, the common misconceptions that plague society at large seem even more entrenched in the Hispanic community. I assumed the burden and privilege of educating everyone and anyone I came across. The misconceptions I heard ranged from offensive to ridiculous. I explained that having a glass of wine during pregnancy did not cause

Down syndrome; same goes for using a microwave, being outside during a lunar eclipse, and people giving my tummy the evil eye. I lost track of how many times I detailed what Down syndrome is and what it is not. I explained how a child with this disability is like other "normal" children. "Kids are kids," I'd say. Children with Down syndrome are playful; they like to imitate other children; they love ice cream, watching movies, listening to music, and so forth. I realized that educating Latinos about Down syndrome was not something I could continue to do casually. The need for an educational effort was monumental, to say the least, and I decided to begin by acting locally.

Finding FUERZA

I met Maria Richardson during the first National Down Syndrome Congress that Alex and I attended. Maria's son also had Down syndrome and was fifteen years old when Eric was only a few weeks old. I admired how adept she was at taking care of her son. When we first met, there was an instantaneous connection, and we left the conference feeling like old friends. We promised to keep in touch. Time and time again, she would prove to be a fountain of inspiration and a pillar of support. She probably sensed my need for guidance. Every now and then she'd call, but more often than not, I was the one who called her with updates on Eric and to ask her questions. She had a gentle nature; I wasn't surprised to find out that she was a peer counselor for parents caring for children with Down syndrome. She was also a regular member of the Down Syndrome Association of Los Angeles.

From our initial meeting onward, we kept on returning to the need to educate people who only spoke Spanish on Down syndrome. I attended the English-only, monthly meetings of the Down Syndrome Association of Los Angeles; these took place during weeknights and in different locations. Not only did participants have to understand English, but they also needed to have the ability to drive to these meetings. Maria and I had no problems with these requirements, but what about the rest of our community? The language barrier coupled with a lack of transportation were often insurmountable barriers. Something needed to be done.

When Eric was just over a year old, Maria and I decided to move forward with a potential support group specifically for Spanish speakers. We brainstormed about where to begin and decided to send out thirty invitations to families who only spoke Spanish. We decided to hold our meetings in a classroom within St. Matthias Catholic Church because we knew the majority of our community wouldn't feel intimidated by meeting in a church. Father Rody Gorman applauded our initiative in forming a group that had never existed and said that he'd help us in any way he could. After some research, we discovered that we were the only Down syndrome group nationwide that catered directly to Spanish speakers. This was back in 1986; now there are many more such groups.

Although we had a hunch that there was a need for a support group, it still surprised us when twenty people showed up. I remember explaining to them that Maria and I didn't need a Spanish support group because we spoke English and were already members of another support group. We let them know that we were willing to set up and run a support group if they felt it would benefit them. We were trying to gage their genuine interest and commitment before pumping our energy into its creation. There was an overwhelmingly positive response and we decided to call it Padres de Personas con Sindrome Down (Parents of Persons with Down Syndrome). It wasn't until 1991 that we renamed the group FUERZA, or "strength." We had monthly meetings and developed a year-long plan that included: inviting professionals in the field to talk with us, training sessions for parents to become peer counselors, a gathering for siblings, and a summer picnic. Our goal was set: to become the premier support group for Latino families of children with Down syndrome.

I never felt so alive with purpose. I was brimming with energy and ideas. Having left my position at the bank, I could dedicate myself exclusively to Eric and building our support group. The main hurdle was finding the money to finance the group. For a couple of years, we were able to stay afloat with an annual budget of two thousand dollars. This money was used to cover phone expenses, copies, and the mailing of the bimonthly newsletters that I wrote. It was a labor of love. The board of directors usually pitched in a few dollars and local businesspeople did the same. I still remember the shock when we received our first five-hundred-dollar donation from the Southern California Gas Company. This struck the entire group as such a generous act. It financed our first symposium and, in a way, validated our efforts. We felt like we must be on to something special to receive this much support.

At the national level, October is National Down Syndrome Month. Traditionally, support groups across the nation hold programs to further the cause of those who have this disability. Activities usually include: symposiums, conferences, walkathons, fund-raising activities, and the National Down Syndrome Congress. When our group met to discuss how we would celebrate, various ideas floated around, but then it hit us: Why not have a mass dedicated to our children? After all, the church had generously provided us with a meeting location. We knew we could utilize the power of the pulpit to educate Latino parents about the value of their children and the programs available to support their families. What better way to communicate our message in Spanish than through the influential cultural medium of the church?

Three hundred people attended our first mass in 1986. It was an incredible turnout and every year the number of attendees grows, now reaching over a thousand. For our second annual mass, we invited Archbishop (now Cardinal) Roger Mahoney. We were honored that he agreed to celebrate the gift of our children with us. I vividly remember the offertory. A number of children with Down syndrome walked down the aisle with their offerings of wine, bread, grapes, and flowers, and then—much to our surprise—the archbishop knelt down to receive the offerings from the children's hands. We were all humbled to witness the highest authority of our church paying homage to our children by bowing down before them. The whole experience augured well for future success.

One quiet evening, after Eric was already asleep, my husband and I were on the couch when a thought rippled through me with a visceral thrill.

"I know exactly what my mission in life is going to be." I gripped Alex's hand.

"Well, what is it?" he asked.

"I'm going to leave this world a better place for people like Eric and families like ours."

"Well, *mamacita* [my mother], if that's your mission in life, then mine will be to ensure that you accomplish yours."

It was that simple. In a moment, my life's mission came to me with sparkling clarity. As a bonus, my husband pledged his support.

It has been many years since that conversation took place. Alex has been my steady hand—an endless source of quiet and unwavering support. He has honored his commitment with dignity. I couldn't have asked for a better partner, friend, and husband. I've always said that we were made for each other. I knew from the first time I laid eyes on him that I'd marry him—mine was love at first sight. He's admitted to me that his was not. I'm guessing that I must have grown on him. We've been married for twenty-five years and with each passing day my love for him grows deeper. The young love we've shared has grown into a wonderfully mature love. The kind of love that could only come from meeting challenges together. Through it all, he has been my strongest advocate in my goal to leave the world a better place for people like Eric.

Sure, this sounded like a noble goal pursuit, but what exactly would it mean? How could it be measured? I didn't exactly know what I should do next, or what tangible objectives needed to be set. Nevertheless, the purity of my intention was undeniable. There was a sense of peace about my newfound raison d'être. I'd use the most basic values as my guide. I reasoned that as long as my mission was clear, the path to accomplish it would reveal itself in time. I was certain that I'd become an instrument through which a calling much greater than my child, my family, or myself could be realized. I willfully submitted to my growing conviction. My life was filled with purposeful action. I was ready to confront a host of challenges that were waiting just around the bend—each with its own inherent lesson to teach.

PART TWO

A
Political Life

7. Bridging Two Worlds

The events and opportunities of my life have required that I constantly reinvent myself. Working as a receptionist for City National Bank, I never imagined wanting to be anything other than a banking official. There were numerous aspects to the banking business that I loved. Interacting with customers on a daily basis and providing them with services that could help them was rewarding. While at the bank, I helped small independent banks compete with larger banks by encouraging them to become members of our Instant Teller Network—a network of automated teller machines that would be able to provide the same level of service that the multibranch banks had. Of course, this was back in 1982 when ATM machines weren't as ubiquitous as they are today. My future in banking lay before me like a detailed spreadsheet that predicted professional growth.

Then, of course, Eric came into my life and required that I redefine what my future would look like and what truly mattered to me. I can't stress enough how important it is to have a strong purpose and mission in life. I knew that I would sleep soundly and feel fulfilled just by doing the smallest things to help make the world better for people like Eric. That is when and why I poured all my energy into FUERZA. It became apparent that this volunteer business was far more time-consuming and complicated than I ever anticipated. It was difficult to travel monthly to Sacramento to protect the rights and advocate for services for people with disabilities, when at home I had a family that relied heavily on me. I was exhausted, but fulfilled.

Meanwhile, the 1990 campaign for governor in California was over. I was pleased to see that Pete Wilson was elected. I followed the race closely to understand where the candidates stood on issues involving people with disabilities. As a mother of a child with a disability, I trusted my gut and intuition. While some people may not be able to discern a difference between pity and compassion, I could tell within seconds by how people approached my son. When asked about people with disabilities during his campaign, Pete Wilson always demonstrated compassion. I approved of him immediately. In my mind, it was very simple: if you cared about people like my son, then you were bound to care about everyone else.

My level of political involvement up until that point was exclusively as a mother battling for the rights of those with disabilities. My efforts were nonpartisan and fueled only by the needs of the people I cared the most about. I became the consummate advocate by attending rallies and media events, testifying in legislative hearings, and assuming the unofficial position of spokesperson for the Hispanic community. I was often described by community activists and newspapers as the Hispanic voice within the disabled community. I was proud to know that attention was being paid to our causes.

I had served as a member of Area Board X on Developmental Disabilities for a few years when my friend Eileen Cassidy, the executive director, found out that Dennis Amundson—someone we highly approved of—was being considered by Governor-Elect Wilson to become the new director of the Department of Developmental Services. Denny had been instrumental in shepherding the Lanterman Act into law—a law that would give great protections to people with disabilities.

Eileen and I wasted no time in setting up a meeting to speak with Denny. We wanted to talk to him about his plans for the Department of Developmental Services, if he came to be its director. To this day, Denny swears that it was this conversation with us that truly challenged and tested him. At our meeting, Denny proved to be a wonderful candidate for the position; he spoke articulately about his commitment to advance the agenda for people with disabilities. He was clearly able to outline his plans that sprung from a deep-rooted knowledge in the field. His compassion for the people I cared most about was something that could not be faked. Both Eileen and I were impressed and hoped that he would become the new director.

To our excitement, shortly after our meeting, Denny became the new director. Within days of his appointment, he called to ask whether I'd be interested in joining the administration as the chief of legislative affairs for the Department of Developmental Services. After recovering from the initial shock, I clarified things for Denny:

"Me? Don't you see I'm pregnant, Denny? Besides, I'm just a mom. How could I be in the governor's administration? I don't know anything about government!" I was pregnant with Alex, and Eric and Carmen needed their mother.

"Rosario, all that is irrelevant to me. The bottom line is that you've been more successful in advocating for people with disabilities than anyone I know, myself included."

"I just don't know. My life is hectic right now and—"

"As a mother, you have tremendous credibility. No one in his right mind would ever challenge your sincerity or knowledge of the system. You know you're the right woman for this position."

"Thank you, Denny, for the invitation and your faith in me, but there's just no . . . I mean with my third child on the way and—"

"Listen, all I'm asking is that you just think about it," he said. "Give it some time to sink in."

I said good-bye, hung up the phone, and didn't give it another thought. How could I when I knew the position would require that I move the entire family six hours away to Sacramento—or even worse, leave them behind in Huntington Park.

A few months later, Alex was born. My husband could only help out so much, given his full-time job and school. My hands were full. My mother began to help me with taking care of my children. In the meantime, Denny visited Los Angeles and told me that the position was still waiting. He informed me that five people tried for the position, but not one made it through the appointment process. "It's clear as day that this job was made for you." He jokingly knelt down on his knee. "It is preordained, Rosario."

Although it was meant as a joke, there was a tinge of truth that resonated with me. What if Denny was right? What if the fact that five people had tried for the position and failed was a sign? Maybe this was indeed what God wanted me to do. Maybe this was a part of my life's mission. Hesitantly, I promised Denny that I'd think some more about it.

My husband and I discussed the matter for a long time, turning it over in our minds and considering it from every angle. I made it clear that I had never sought this position, that I never even thought about working for a governor, never mind occupying a position that offered the ability to change laws. Considering the potential sacrifices both individually and as a family was overwhelming. Both my husband and I came from tight-knit families that acted as our unconditional support system; neither of us had been away from them for an extended period of time. I knew my mother would have great difficulty accepting it. The last time my family had been separated was when we first moved to the U.S. Besides, how would Eric respond to the move? We'd have to sell our beautiful house in order to afford buying a new one in Sacramento. Then—in order for us to stay together as a family—my husband would have to leave his job and find a new one. There were too many considerations.

After agonizing over the decision, we both acknowledged it would be an opportunity to enact real change in the lives of families like ours. We concluded there was no harm done in applying for the position. At least that way, there wouldn't be any lingering doubts in my mind. On the other hand, if I applied and was offered the position, then perhaps it really was meant to be. Either way, we'd cross that bridge *if* we came to it. I continually asked God to guide me. If this were his will, then I'd submit to it. If not, I was more than happy to continue to stay at home with the children.

On the flight from Los Angeles to my interview in Sacramento, I became skeptical about my chances of being selected: *Why would I get this position if five other people already tried for it and didn't? Besides, I'm just a mom. . . .* I submitted my application and was interviewed by Kim Belshe, Jeannie Cain, and Terri Steffan from the Health and Welfare Agency. I left their office without the air of confidence that accompanies a successful interview. I felt that being absent from the work world for a few years had made me lose my edge. I told my husband I was certain I did not make the cut. We were both satisfied and, admittedly, a bit relieved—this was obviously not meant to be.

Then the next day our phone rang.

"Congratulations, Rosario, you've made it through the agency!" Denny's excitement exuded from the phone.

"But, how is that possible?"

"I told you, this is preordained," Denny said. "Now you need to get ready for the interview with the governor's office."

I was in disbelief when I hung up the phone; my heart was racing.

A few days later, I found myself in the lobby of the governor's office. While waiting to be interviewed, I breathed deeply. The whole scene seemed surreal. I went through the motions of another interview as though on autopilot. I shook hands with Julie Justus—the appointments secretary—who carried a folder with several newspaper articles jutting out.

She mentioned that she had read a few stories where my efforts were featured prominently. Throughout the interview, Julie was kind, inquisitive, but ultimately noncommittal. I was certainly not getting the go-ahead to ask if I was going to be offered the position. I didn't even dare finish the interview with the "When do I start?" question.

On my flight back home to Los Angeles, even more questions sprouted. What if this actually happened? Was this the right thing for me to do? Would I be in a better position to help people with disabilities? Was pursuing this position in the best interest of my family? The flight attendant gave me a concerned look and I realized I was sobbing.

The next day brought another phone call.

"Congratulations. Once again, you made it through," Denny said. "Now, I hope that your background is squeaky clean."

"What does that mean?" I asked.

"It means that if—I mean, *when* you make it through, I'll be talking with the next chief of legislative affairs," he said.

"Denny, I live across the street from St. Martha's Church; when I hang up the phone with you, I'm going to walk across the street and pray. If this is God's will, then I'll join you in Sacramento."

I hung up the phone and went to church. Kneeling down near the altar, I prayed: "Dear God, please help me to know if this is the right decision for my family. Not just for me, but for everyone. You know I didn't even seek this position. It came to me. I have a good life here with my family. Is leaving them and my mom really what I should do? Is this the price I have to pay to serve a greater purpose?"

At the end of my prayer, I felt a peace in my heart—it was out of my hands for now.

It all happened so quickly after that. I was offered the position and decided to seize the opportunity. The press release from the governor's office announcing my appointment was distributed a few weeks later. The anticipation of starting in my new position was simultaneously exhilarating and frightening.

In a matter of days, I smoothly handed over the administration of FUERZA to the board of directors, more specifically to my friend Maria Zaragoza, who became the organization's president. Then came the more difficult part: figuring out what was best for my family. My husband and I decided that I'd make the move to Sacramento first before transplanting the whole family. We hired a wonderful woman named Flori to help us with the children. It wasn't long before Flori became a part of the family, always in attendance at birthdays, communions, and other important events. My first few months in Sacramento would be devoted to establishing myself in my new role, renting an apartment, and helping my husband search for a new position. Once those items were checked off the to-do list, we'd put our house in Huntington Park up for sale and use that money to buy a new place in Sacramento.

For the first few months, I'd leave on Mondays and return on Fridays. Although emotionally difficult, it seemed like a feasible four-to-six-month plan. With any luck we'd be reunited even sooner than that. The first time I left my family, I was struck with a feeling of both sadness and recognition. I wondered if this was, to some extent, what it had felt like for my father when he left us behind in Mexico. Now it was my family that was divided in hopes of greater opportunities and a greater cause.

I'll forever be indebted to my friend Eileen Cassidy who provided a roof over my head while I settled in Sacramento. We both worked for the Department of Developmental Services and having a friendly face to come home to made my transition much easier.

My family's four-to-six-month plan devolved into a modified one-year plan. The economy had taken a turn for the worse and our house in Huntington Park hadn't sold. As the weeks passed, it became more difficult to leave my husband and children. Sunday nights were dreadful; all I could think about was having to leave my family again the next morning. We took the house off the market and then put it back on. We lowered the asking price. Months passed with nobody showing interest.

Back in Sacramento, I completely immersed myself in work and it began to bear fruit. I was the first to arrive in the office (usually before seven) and was often the last to leave around seven or eight in the evening; the janitors were my nightly companions. I, of course, thought of my dad, who as a janitor would do his work when everyone was gone for the day. The roars of the nightly vacuums only strengthened my resolve. My dad's work ethic powered me day after day. I was determined to make sure that I lived up to the example and sacrifices my parents had made. I worked myself to exhaustion each single day, arriving home with just enough energy to microwave popcorn and plop myself in front of the television.

During that first year that I was in Sacramento, Governor Pete Wilson signed the most sweeping legislative reform of the past twenty years that would impact people with disabilities. This was a huge success for advocates who had pushed this legislation for years. I was proud to be a member of the blue ribbon committee that made recommendations. Now, as chief of legislative affairs, it was my analysis that the governor read to sign or veto the legislation. Of course, it was the product of a tremendous team effort that involved individuals, groups, legislators, and staff at the department to finally see this result. When the governor signed the legislation, we all breathed a tremendous sigh of relief. Now, more than ever, I felt I was at the right place at the right time. It was a privilege to be part of a historic milestone for the entire disability system; it was work that would cause reverberations throughout the entire nation. And to think I was in the middle of it all.

In 1992—when I had been in my position for nearly a year—the state was facing extreme budget cuts. The budget gap was fourteen billion dollars and the governor was proposing seven billion in government spending cuts and seven billion in tax increases. As part of the administration, my job was to advance Governor Wilson's legislative priorities while tracking all pieces of legislation that could potentially affect people with disabilities. These were two goals that rarely came into conflict. Of course, rarely doesn't mean never.

With such drastic cuts, there was simply no way to get around the fact that every state program would be altered. Denny, like every department head, was charged with developing a set of proposed cuts for our department to show to the governor. With Denny having to go away for a couple of days, he set his executive committee to work on formulating the proposals, legislative language, and the department's proposed budget.

I received a copy of the complete proposal. I read the document with great care, flipping through pages and pages of legislative language that detailed changes and possible cuts. And then, a single lined jumped out and punched me in the gut. Although I don't remember the exact wording, it essentially boiled down to a beheading of the disability system. I felt robbed of all our hard work. The language made it clear that services for people with disabilities would be denied, except in cases of imminent health problems leading to death.

To put this in an appropriate context, let me suggest that the system for people with disabilities in California is widely regarded as one of the nation's best. California assumes responsibility for its citizens with disabilities from the cradle to the grave. These changes would have obliterated it. Devastated, I thought of any possible way I could stop this. By the time Denny returned, the proposal would be overdue. There was simply no way that he'd have enough time to read the entire report word for word after it made its rounds. Before taking any hasty action, I thought through my options and felt it best to seek out advice.

Part of my duties included lobbying legislators on behalf of the Department of Developmental Services. A few weeks prior to reading the proposal, I had made an appointment to meet an assemblywoman. Walking into her office, my legs began to wobble. I knew that I wasn't going to be able to discuss any legislation with the department's budget proposal consuming all my thoughts. I needed guidance and perhaps she could help, I thought. Without going into any details of my predicament, I asked how she handled difficult situations. I explained that I was at the end of my rope and wasn't sure what kind of knot I should tie before hanging on.

"I can see you're distressed, Rosario," she said. "But since I know you can't give me any of the specifics of your situation, let me relay something that has always helped me."

I perked up, hoping that what she was about to say would somehow lead me down the right path.

"I always draw a line and promise myself that no matter what, I will not cross it," she said simply. "That also means that I never move the line to accommodate my current situation because that's the same thing as crossing the line. I'm also careful not to come up with excuses for moving the line. Once you do that, then you have to ask yourself, when will I stop?"

It took a moment for her advice to sink in and to see how it translated into my situation. Like the best advice, hers was simple and yet helped tremendously.

"Thank you so much for your advice and time," I said. "I know what I must do now."

My line was drawn: there was no way I'd continue to

work for the DDS if the proposal moved forward. I would not waver in helping those with disabilities. I had to accept the reality that if I lost this fight, I would hand in my resignation. I talked to my husband over the phone and he agreed with my decision. I was in pain over the turn of events, but I wasn't conflicted. Drawing my line had granted me serenity. I had to be true to what I cherished.

Denny returned in the late afternoon of the next day. I approached him immediately. My predicament rested heavily on my shoulders and the sooner I understood where he stood, the better. Although there was no one left on the floor at that late hour, I asked Denny if I could close his door.

"What's wrong?" he asked.

"Have you seen the proposed language for the budget cuts?" I asked, attempting to control the tremble in my voice.

"To be honest, I haven't had a chance to review it."

I saw the proposal lying in his in-box and grabbed it.

"Let me guide you to the most offensive part then," I said.

I gave Denny a few minutes to read through the paragraph. After what seemed like an eternity, he looked up at me. I was content to see an angered expression animate his face.

"I simply cannot accept this and live with myself," I said. "I didn't come to Sacramento to destroy the system that protects people like my son. That's not why *we* came to this department, Denny. I'm going to have to resign this moment if—"

"Rosario, that won't be necessary," he said. "First of all, thank you for bringing this to my attention. Second, I'm assuming that you'll attend the meeting I'm holding first thing in the morning."

The impromptu meeting was held the next morning. There was the murmur of everyone asking what the heck this surprise meeting was about. Among coffee mugs, notebooks, and pens was the proposal lying in the middle of the table.

"I'm holding this meeting today to ask you why we all work here." Denny looked around the table at puzzled faces. "Well, let me remind you that we are here to fight for people with disabilities."

Inside, I was jumping for joy.

"Now, I know we need to make cuts, but if this"—Denny lifted the proposal and let it drop again—"is the best you can do, then you don't deserve to work in this department."

I know that many of my colleagues were caught off guard by Denny's indignation and were perplexed by how quickly he focused in on the specific language that needed to be addressed. As the committee turned to the proposal with fresh eyes, discussion began immediately.

As a mother, I will be eternally indebted to Denny, and as an advocate, I'll forever admire his abilities. I always knew his heart was in the right place, but time and time again, he went beyond the call of duty and became the biggest champion for our cause. He fought with every weapon in his political arsenal for our budget. This was personal. Denny had spent years working hard with the author of the initial bill that created the law that was now on the chopping block.

After all of our efforts, our department was not only

spared the anticipated cuts, but the governor increased our budget to accommodate the growth in the number of people with disabilities relying on the system. Denny and I couldn't be more satisfied with the news. On a personal level, it was satisfying to know that all the sacrifices—like leaving my family each week—were not in vain. Denny had been right: I was given an opportunity to make a positive difference in the lives of those with disabilities and that was now coming to fruition.

Our success inspired us to achieve even more the following year. As a result of our team's efforts, we had the governor sign into law the California Early Intervention Services Act. This was a piece of legislation that finally focused on the big picture: the needs of both the children and their families. Prior to this law, only the needs of the child with disabilities, independent of the family setting, were considered. Our new law called for changes in the programming of services to account for the differences in families. For the first time, for instance, if a single mother had more than one child, a full-time job, and the need to take her child to a variety of specialists, her situation was considered on a different level from that of someone who didn't have all these added challenges. The result would help thousands of existing families as well as new families coming into the system for the first time.

By this point, I couldn't have been more satisfied professionally with my place in the administration. I had been an instrumental part of reforming the entire system. As a mother of a child with disabilities, I felt honored to be in a position that allowed me to play a role in preserving and improving the system for thousands of children like Eric. I was confident that in spite of its imperfections, California still had the most comprehensive system for protecting the rights of people with developmental disabilities.

Unfortunately, it was coming up on two years and our house in Huntington Park hadn't sold. We took it off and put it back on the market twice and still nothing. Our hopes of moving the family to Sacramento were quickly waning. There was no getting around the fact that the real estate market was dead, and we couldn't afford a new place without selling the old. The emotional price my family was paying for my absence had been well worth the results, but it was unsustainable. It was torture to leave my children each week. I still have vivid memories of those Monday mornings when Carmen would cling to my leg and cry. The entire family dreaded these weekly departures; it was always the same ritual and it was also becoming more difficult to focus on my work when I knew my children were growing up so quickly and needed me. My husband and I tried to come up with new rationalizations with each passing week, but the writing was on the wall: it was time to return to my family.

When I took a moment to reflect, I was confident that I had accomplished what I had set out to do in my position as the chief of legislative affairs for the DDS. I could take a deep breath and rest assured that my mission in Sacramento was complete: people like Eric and families like ours would be better off. The protections the new laws afforded them were significant; the new programs would make their lives much easier.

I made the announcement shortly after my husband and I decided that moving back was indeed the best option for us as a family. Although everyone was sad to see me go, they understood. The governor asked if I could stay in his administration as an appointed member of the State Council on Developmental Disabilities. The council's main role is to develop the state plan to serve its citizens with disabilities. I was elated because even though it was an unpaid position, it allowed me to continue to work on the issues I was passionate about.

I was extremely honored and fortunate to be selected as the council's chair almost immediately; I'd ultimately serve on the council for more than two years. During that time, our most important effort was to ensure the continuation of federal funding. There were times when the federal government threatened to withhold funding—and this was unacceptable. Luckily, we were able to work with the commissioner on developmental disabilities and ensure the continued funding if we agreed to complete some of the tasks they proposed, like rearranging how the state was allocating federal funds. A state program should not be funded with federal dollars. In the end, everyone was content; I was beginning to believe in happy endings while I looked forward to the next chapter of my life.

8. Acting Locally

Opportunity came knocking again as I was tying up loose ends and packing my bags to head back home permanently to my family in Huntington Park. I couldn't wait to be a regular part of the kids' lives again. At the same time, Raul Perez, a sitting city council member in Huntington Park, was attending a League of California Cities conference in Sacramento. He stopped in my office to deliver an intriguing bit of local political news. One of the current council members was not running for reelection and since he, Raul, was, he needed someone to run with him on the same slate. Given my experience in Sacramento, he believed I'd be a great candidate.

After considering what he was asking, I agreed that my experience in Sacramento had prepared me well to serve on a council position. However, there was one major consideration: I had never run for an elected office. To have a chance at winning, I was going to need a lot of help.

The timing of this opportunity was too perfect and made me wonder if it was also part of a larger plan. I began to think that as long as I worked hard, I'd be blessed with opportunities. Again, I wasn't looking for this opportunity, but it would be an excellent way to continue my public service, and in *mi comunidad*. It didn't matter that my salary would be reduced significantly. Prior to this news, I was ready to stay home full-time with my children. As luck would have it, this was a part-time position. I couldn't imagine a more perfect scenario.

As is always the case when facing a great challenge, I began to pray. It's my tried-and-true way of quieting all the white noise and connecting with a higher power. I knew that, if elected, it would be a significant investment of time and energy. I also felt the common fear and apprehension that go with tackling anything unfamiliar. Raul listened to my concerns and reassured me that he'd teach me everything I needed to know about running a campaign. "After all, I had to learn *something* from my six prior losses. You'll have the benefit of my experience." This calmed me, but I wouldn't even consider losing. If I was going to do this, then I had to win.

My family welcomed me back home with open arms. I got to catch up on quality time with my husband and children. Having their support as I ran for city council was all I could ask for. I knew, however, that to even have a chance at being elected, I'd need to seek political support.

I was advised to meet with Joe Valverde. He was known as the first stop for anyone seriously considering a political career in Huntington Park. Even though Joe didn't live in Huntington Park, anyone who was anyone in local politics had gone to him at some point. To put it simply, he was the kingmaker. He was intimately involved with the United

States Junior Chamber (Jaycees) for years. This nonprofit organization for young people focuses on building leadership through community volunteerism and is often considered a launching pad for many politicians, giving them opportunities to make beneficial professional connections.

Thinking of the adage that there's no better way to a man's heart than through his stomach, I made a reservation at Dal Rae Restaurant in Pico Rivera for our meeting. Joe arrived promptly and we began our delicious meal, talking about anything other than the original premise for our meeting. Joe's mild eyes and hearty laugh put me at ease; we had good chemistry. As we were finishing up the meal—amid the clinking of silverware—there was a dead silence. Joe turned serious.

"What would you say if I told you that you just don't have what it takes to become a council member?" he asked plainly.

I was taken aback and felt a piece of food catch in my throat. I thought I had prepared myself for anything he could throw my way, but I never expected those words to tumble out of his mouth. I searched Joe's face for any clue that he was kidding. What I saw was a man with a blank expression and a salt-and-pepper crew cut. I took a deep breath and tried not to get angry.

"So, I repeat, Rosario. What would you—"

"I'll tell you what," I interrupted, "I'd go home and plan a way to prove you wrong!" All of a sudden I felt like I was back in school with all the children laughing at my supposedly low IQ. Having to prove myself had fueled me once before and this time would be no different.

"Seriously?" He chuckled.

"Of course. I'm going to go home and develop a plan to make sure I get into the council," I continued calmly. "And then I'll invite you to my swearing in."

"Interesting." Joe seemed to be an expert at one-word jabs.

"Joe, with all due respect, I'm going to do this even if you think I shouldn't."

"That a girl! You have the bug!" he said, eyes beaming. "I was just testing you to see if you had what it takes to become a council member."

I laughed with great relief.

"Don't worry, you have my support," he said, "and I'll be in the front row when you're getting sworn in."

With our main business off the table, Joe began to share memories of past races. He spoke of the many people who came to him for support with expectations that all they had to do was declare their candidacy and he'd do the heavy lifting. It was clear to him that I did not fall into that category, since I was ready to go it alone. Proving to him that I wasn't relying on his support, he in turn granted me that support. He proceeded to give me some advice that would continue to serve me for many years to come—and not just in local politics. It was clear to me that he was a wise man. The rest of our conversation circled around whether I was not only ready, but also serious about entering the world of politics. Before we parted, Joe promised to spread the word about my running for the city council seat.

There are many sayings in politics, but there is one that arises with great frequency: "In politics, friends come and go but enemies only accumulate." Although I have my fair share of enemy accumulation, I disagree. It goes against my nearly two decades of experience in politics with a list of friends that continues to grow. Joe Valverde was the first of many. In the years that followed, he became not only my advisor, but also a true, unyielding friend.

Not too long ago, Joe was being recognized at a luncheon and I had the honor of toasting him. I can't remember the exact words I used but I hope it conveyed how appreciative I am of his role in my life. While he showed me that in politics you can have allies, he also stressed the importance of keeping relationships in perspective. Today someone may agree with you on a specific issue and tomorrow he or she may be your opponent on another issue. The important thing is not to take it personally: that's just the way it is. With Joe's advice, I've been able to evolve many political relationships into enduring friendships.

In March of 1994, I was elected to the city council seat. There were about nine people running for three positions. It was then that I realized that in local politics, the smaller the stakes, the higher the passions. Although Latinos constituted over 80 percent of the population of the city of Huntington Park, this was the first time they would also be a super majority in the council, with four Latino members. The first two Latino members were elected in 1990 and the third was appointed in 1993 after a longtime council member passed away. I was the fourth. With the council reflecting the diversity of the community in which we lived, the hope was that real change would occur.

The Great Divide: Proposition 187

I would learn the true meaning of being caught in a Catch-22 when Proposition 187 was being fiercely debated in California. If passed, any and all public services to people who were in California illegally would be denied. This even applied to schooling for children and medical care for people with disabilities (the only exception being emergencies). The implications of this proposition were unacceptable to me. The path I needed to walk to stay true to my convictions would leave me without friends for a while; it was a necessary lesson that taught me that, even when no one else is standing behind you, the strength of your convictions will sustain you.

Proposition 187 would stir all of Californians' emotions and harshly divide the political landscape. Charges and countercharges of racism were leveled every day. The airwaves were plagued with accusations that the "illegals" were to blame for all of society's ills. On the other end of the spectrum, advocates of the "undocumented" painted them as the saviors of our society. This debate was occurring days after I had been elected to the council. In a city whose population consisted mostly of Democratic Latinos and thousands of both documented and undocumented immigrants, the overwhelming majority of Huntington Park was against the proposition. I felt torn. On the one hand, as a representative of the people of my city, I had a duty to represent their opposition. Politically, however, I was an appointee of Governor Pete Wilson, who was for the proposition but had also been extremely supportive of the bills on behalf of people with disabilities; he was pivotal in signing the most sweeping reform in decades. The lines between the political and personal can sometimes blur. I decided to take a brave stand: I supported the governor in his reelection, but I opposed Proposition 187.

People didn't know what to make of me. The Republicans, while appreciative of my support for the governor's reelection, were also upset that I opposed the initiative. The opposite held true for the Democrats, who applauded my opposition to the initiative but were angered that I was supporting the governor. This was the first of several times that I'd find myself alone because of being on the "wrong side" of an issue. The division was so strong that it became increasingly difficult to have a regular conversation with anyone. But by myself, I stood stronger.

I had come to the conclusion that despite Proposition 187, the governor was the superior candidate. I had witnessed firsthand how he deftly dealt with the state's fiscal challenges. The policies he set in motion helped to turn around California's economy. This coupled with other considerations led me to believe that he deserved to be reelected. Supporting him did not mean, however, that—under any circumstance—I could support something like taking children out of school because they were in California without documents.

In my view the children should not be fodder for political debate. The commercials that were running for Proposition 187 were downright despicable. Filmed in black and white (an attempt, I assumed, to convey a documentary's seriousness), they panned across a classroom of children that were obviously Latino. The not-so-subliminal message was that *these* children shouldn't receive a taxpayer-funded education. As a mother watching this commercial, I'd be hard-pressed to find anything more offensive on such a deeply personal level.

A few days later, I was asked to attend a meeting with people from the governor's reelection campaign. The meeting was to be held after working hours at the headquarters in Sacramento. They needed all the support they could find. California was still dealing with the aftermath of one of the most difficult recessions in recent history and the reelection campaign was expected to be challenging. I was one of several Latino appointees brought together to discuss the governor's recent announcement of support for Proposition 187; the plan was for the proposition campaign to be in full swing during the last six weeks leading up to the election. A meeting was called to hear our reactions and to ask for our support.

Quite a few Latino appointees showed up. The governor's team briefed us on the reelection campaign: where the governor stood, the polls, the opposition, and so forth. I could see on my colleagues' faces that this was a difficult meeting. When asked my point of view, I simply stated my full support of the governor's reelection. But that didn't mean supporting Proposition 187, the governor's team understood me.

Walking Through the Political Minefield

As the campaign for the governor's reelection continued to heat up, two forces continuously collided against each other.

The line was sharply drawn: either you were for Proposition 187 and the governor's reelection or you were against both. The gray area on either side of this line was dotted with political mines.

One day, an influential Democratic Party member met with me and suggested that the governor was not the right candidate for the Latino community. She also said that should the proposition pass, it would hurt our community *very* badly. She asked that I renounce my party affiliation and support the governor's opponent during an upcoming press conference. If I did this, I could count on becoming an assemblywoman at the earliest possible election. She seemed to have my entire political future mapped out.

I was in shock at what she was even suggesting. It took me a few moments to reply. "Not only will I have nothing to do with this deal, I'm offended you've even made the offer." What led her to believe that I'd even consider such an action? I refreshed her memory on how the governor had done everything I had hoped to make the lives for those with disabilities better—that included Latinos, too.

I abruptly brought our conversation to a conclusion: "I'm going home and forgetting we ever had this conversation. Not for even one second will I consider what you asked me to do."

"Mark my words," she said. "I'll make sure you never go beyond your little city council!"

And that was just one minefield . . . pow!

When I arrived home, I immediately told my husband Alex what had happened. What I found most troubling was what their impression of me must have been if they thought I'd even consider becoming a turncoat.

"You can't blame them for trying," he said. "It's politics and they know there are plenty of people who'd jump at an opportunity for self-promotion."

I saw his point. I remembered Joe's words to never take anything in politics personally.

"Their only mistake was in choosing you," Alex concluded.

9. The Judas Kiss

While the race for governor continued, I faced my first political betrayal. I thought back to when I left Sacramento to seek my first elective office and my roommate said: "In politics, trust no one, not even me." She said it with the finality that I now know comes from experience. The statement struck me like a kick to the gut. How could I not trust her, she was my roommate. Being a trusting person, I have never been paranoid about backstabbing. With me, you start at 100 percent and it's your decision to come down from there.

Regrettably, my roommate's warning rang in my ears more times than I care to recall as people that I initially believed to be friends showed their true colors. Nothing serves a better lesson than when you are betrayed for the first time. Thinking so little of the person who betrayed me, I have decided not to mention his name. In parts of Mexico, one is to never utter the name of a dead person. In my eyes, this double-crosser's behavior was so despicable that he *is* dead to me. Besides, why sully my book?

Due to various reelections and the death of one longtime

member, Latinos became the majority—four out of five—on the city council for the first time in 1994. This was long overdue in a city whose population is almost entirely Latino. All of us were well aware of our duties to the citizens and excited about enacting real change. Our first order of business was tackling the crime issues that had plagued our city for too long. The three of us were inseparable: if you saw one of us at a grand opening, political event, or any other function, then you saw us all.

Of course, as council members we had to abide by open meeting laws (the Brown Act). This law precludes the majority of council members from reaching consensus before our meetings were held. If two of us discussed an item, neither of us could talk to a third member before the official council meeting. We had to make sure to present our issue, discuss, deliberate, and vote in public. We took this rule seriously and followed protocol. Of course, as we were the majority, there were often at least three out of four votes for issues raised; this led to legislation making its way quickly through the process.

The position of mayor in Huntington Park, unlike in some larger cities, is not a position elected at large. Instead, it is a one-year rotating position requiring three out of five votes among council members with a mayor pro tem (essentially a "vice mayor") slated to become mayor the following year. Immediately after I was sworn in, the council voted that I become the mayor pro tem. The mayor began to introduce me not as the mayor pro tem, but as the next mayor of the city. This was a rarity. He would even go so far as to state: "Rosario is going to be the first female mayor in the city of Huntington

Park." Every time I heard those words, my heart raced. Of course, I was flattered. I felt honored that I was going to make history. It was just a matter of waiting for the council reorganization meeting—to be held near the end of the current mayor's term—and we'd reach an important milestone.

As time approached, the excitement became evident during a meeting of the Quota Club (a service club for women) where anticipation of the first woman mayor was all the buzz. I asked my friends to wear pink to the city council meeting where my new role would be announced. I, too, would wear pink among the dark suits of the city council. The power of females in politics would be felt.

A couple of weeks before the election, I was preparing the elegant pink invitations for the council meeting where I would officially become mayor. I wanted all my friends and family to be present for this historic moment. I was just about finished with the sealing of the envelopes, two leaning towers eager to be stamped, when I rose to refill my coffee mug. I picked up the local newspaper and began to casually flip through its pages. With great interest, I started reading an article about the city council. I came across a line that I reread several times; it was something to the effect of: "The city is to reorganize at the next council meeting where the question is: Who will be the next mayor of the city of Huntington Park?"

What did he mean *who*? There was no question about who was going to be the next mayor. Of course *I* was going to be the next mayor. I knew that the reporter had been covering local politics for some time now. Was he sleeping under a rock? I felt a burning sensation in my right hand.

Was I having a heart attack? No, but my hand was trembling and causing hot coffee to run down my arm. I steadied myself before calling Raul's cell phone. "Have you read today's paper?" I launched into conversation without even saying hello. He hadn't. I read the lines that had troubled me into the phone's receiver. "I'm going to make a few phone calls," he said. I could tell from his tone that he was just as bewildered as I was.

Later that afternoon, Raul pulled up in his car and I got in. We were headed to an event for the League of California Cities.

"So, what's going on?" I asked as he came to stop at the light and turned to me.

"Our *friend,* the mayor, is not going to vote for you," he said.

I became light-headed instantly.

"Pull over, Raul," I gulped. "I think I'm going to vomit!"

I was surprised by my visceral reaction to the news. I felt as though I had been poisoned.

"Take a deep breath, Rosario," Raul said in an attempt to calm me down.

"This makes no sense," I continued. "Just last week he introduced me as the first female mayor, and now, now he's not even voting for me?" I was in shock. How could the mayor do this to me, to us, to the community? The past few weeks flashed through my memory. Had I done anything wrong?

"You know, I've known him for so many years and sometimes he just acts weird," Raul said. "No rhyme or reason, he just does unpredictable things."

I had so many questions and no answers: I wanted an explanation. I just kept repeating, "He can't do this! This is outrageous!"

I simply could not reconcile all of the mayor's past actions with the present—they just didn't fit together. What kind of a man was he that he couldn't tell me if he had concerns about my selection? Why did he talk to the press first?

"If he's not voting for me," I found myself sobbing, "then who is he voting for?"

"My guess is that it'd have to be the only Anglo on the council."

"But they hate each other," I said. "How could the mayor even think of making that guy the mayor again?"

The whole situation did not add up. Why did the mayor want the city to go backward instead of forward? If he was going to support the former mayor, whose policies obviously demonstrated a lack of understanding of the changing demographics of the city, then he would be turning the clock of progress back.

I was in no shape to attend the social function we were approaching. Feeling completely vulnerable, I asked Raul to take me back home. I needed time to get a grip on my next course of action. Should I confront him? Should I have people talk to him on my behalf? Even if I did want to talk to him, he most likely had already spoken with another council member and—due to the Brown Act—would not be able to engage me in conversation.

I was so light-headed by the time I walked through my door. I told my husband the news and he was in disbelief. I glanced over at the neat pile of invitations; I wanted them out of my sight, so I threw them into the garage. They'd stay there for months before I could bring myself to throw them out.

As soon as I had calmed down a bit, I decided to call Jim McDowall, one of my most trusted friends who, sadly, has since passed away. He was a pitch-perfect soundboard. He was detached from my situation and could be objective about which actions I should consider taking. After I summarized what had happened, the ever-so-sagacious Jim spoke: "It sounds to me like you got screwed, my dear. This guy is not a man, much less a gentleman. He has displayed no integrity and he is obviously not your friend. Welcome to politics!"

"But what should I do now, Jim?" I asked. "I can't go to the city council meeting."

Jim asked that I just listen and launched into a monologue that I'll forever be grateful for; it was exactly what I needed to hear.

"Oh no, my dear, you're only feeling pain and it is clouding your thinking. You are above him because you have integrity. You have nothing to be ashamed of since you did nothing wrong. Chances are he feels threatened by you and this is the perfect way for him to feel superior."

"But Jim," I interrupted, "what should I do?"

"Let me finish what you need to hear. You want to know what you are going to do? You are going to take this bitter pill and swallow it in public—and you are going to do it with class. You're going to pack those chambers with all of your friends and family. We'll all be witnesses to the moment when he stabs you in the back."

"'We'll'?" I asked. I was touched that he'd fly from Sacramento to lend his support.

"Yes, of course I'll be there for you. And I'll see you take your beating with grace. I guarantee that everyone will be sickened when they see how your so-called friend treats you. You'll come out ahead in that meeting if you leave with your head held high and dry cheeks."

"I just don't know, Jim," I said.

"Don't get me wrong; it'll be difficult, but you can do it," he said. "I'll be right there through the entire circus act. Believe me, you'll come out stronger for this."

I had a lot to ponder once I got off the phone. It was difficult to imagine going through what he was suggesting. I didn't even know how I'd find the energy to get out of bed, let alone be the laughing stock of the city. Meanwhile, my political consultant had gotten hold of what was happening and was outraged. He said that once people had become aware of the mayor's intentions, they began calling his office in attempts to change his mind—all with no success. Not only was the man stubborn, but he also wasn't providing explanations to anyone.

My phone rang incessantly on the Sunday night before the Monday council meeting. It seemed like everyone wanted to offer me his or her opinion about the events that were destined to unfold the next day. I couldn't believe my ears when a man's voice on the other end of the line offered his solution: "Listen, I want you to call the mayor tonight and kiss his ass. Promise him whatever he wants. If you have to get on your knees and beg him for the position, then do it. Making that other guy mayor again will be an embarrassment for our city and community." I tried my best to maintain my composure. I politely said I wouldn't even think of calling the mayor, let alone do the other things he was describing. It was then that I reached a place of peace within myself.

Being calm about the situation didn't, of course, mean that I wasn't in pain over the betrayal. I realized, however, that there was little I could do. I wasn't going to break the law by talking to a third council member. I wasn't going to beg for the position and lose my dignity in the process. Why feed into the mayor's power trip? His need to feel in control was so strong that it was clouding his judgment; he was looking out for his best interest by dividing the council and ensuring that he would be the powerful swing vote. After fully analyzing his behavior, I felt pity for him, but certainly not compassion.

The dreaded day arrived, as I knew it would. I had taken Jim's advice and invited everyone I knew to witness what would be one of my most painful moments in politics. It meant a lot to me that Jim came in from Sacramento. Upon seeing him, I tried my best to conjure up a smile. He patted my shoulder and said, "I have come to bury Caesar." I laughed and a smile cracked; I could always count on Jim for his precise comedic timing in stressful situations.

I fixed that smile to my face as I took a seat in the council chambers. I looked out over the audience and saw so many familiar faces: family, friends, and colleagues. I knew I'd be okay, although my stomach felt otherwise; I finally fully understood the expression of a stomach being in knots. The mayor took the podium and made his announcement: he was not only turning against me, but also against one of his friends that some thought he would endorse. I heard a collective gasp when the mayor finally declared that he was endorsing a man he had once professed to hate to become mayor again. I could see the perplexed faces undulating through the crowd like a wave. The mayor's introducing me around the city as the next mayor, the first female mayor, was still fresh in many minds. The community was outraged and it took every bit of my strength to suppress my true emotions.

It was my turn to speak. I cleared my throat and with as much dignity as I could muster, I read the prepared statement that Jim had helped me craft. I made sure to stress that we must all work together toward improving our city, regardless of who is in power. The words somehow continued to spill out of my mouth while I focused on not breaking down. After I was finished reading my tear-free statement, applause ensued despite the sense of defeat permeating the council chambers.

After the meeting ended, the number of people who approached to let me know how proud they were of me far outnumbered those congratulating the new mayor. At that moment, a poem I had learned as a student in Mexico came rushing back. It's called "A Gloria," or "The Glory," and the applicable part reads: "They can take the victory away from me, but not the glory." Seeing the turn of events, I knew this was indeed true. To some, this might have seemed like a victory, but there was certainly no glory in what went against what the majority wanted. Moving forward, I had to deal courageously with my disappointment and, more importantly, protect the city's image. I knew that my reaction to these events would partly guide the community's response.

A reporter called the next day, looking for the scoop. He admitted to me that he, too, was wondering why the former mayor did what he did. Why, with an opportunity to make history with the first female mayor, he had chosen otherwise.

"So, you must be completely outraged," said the reporter. "Do you have any idea why the former mayor chose not to support you?"

I sensed he was looking for a sensationalized story. He probably assumed I was in a vulnerable state and would offer him something juicy to print. No matter how much people insisted, I would not attack the former mayor or the new mayor.

"Of course I am disappointed by the mayor's actions," I said, almost feeling the anticipation on the other end of the line. "However, I cannot speculate as to the rationale behind his actions. You will have to ask him directly."

The reporter sounded disappointed when the interview concluded. I refused to create a circuslike atmosphere in the council. I had witnessed some of the spectacles within the chambers of surrounding cities and was determined to not have the same occur in ours. My disappointment would not tarnish our city's reputation. I learned a valuable lesson: there are forces with consequences that would often be more important than me. This would be the first of many times that I'd learn to remove myself from a situation in order to understand what was truly important.

For peace of mind, I knew I'd eventually have to get some answers from the former mayor. I let a few weeks pass before I called him.

"Okay, so now that it's all over, can you tell me why you decided not to vote for me?" I asked. He coughed and I could hear the hesitation in his voice.

"There were three reasons," he said.

"I'm listening," I said.

"Do you really want to get into this, Rosario?"

"Yes, actually I do," I said firmly.

He proceeded more or less to tell me that I had let the potential mayor position go to my head. The second reason was his fear that I'd use the position only as leverage for a higher position. The final reason was that I was simply not qualified for the position.

I was silent while processing his rationale. I was even more dumfounded than before I had asked. How could he even begin to say all these things after he originally endorsed me as the next mayor? I never asked for that type of recognition. Second, I had never mentioned to him or to anyone else anything about seeking higher office—the main reason being that I wasn't. Regardless, it is everyone's right to seek a higher office. Okay, for some reason he was pulling these reasons out of thin air, but it was his last reason—that I wasn't qualified—that was truly offensive. I didn't understand what gave him the authority to pass judgment on my experience when his was as a schoolteacher. Interestingly, his qualifications for office were never questioned.

I could have filled the silence on the other end of the line with a rundown of my resume: I had worked for a bank, created a nonprofit organization, and helped change state laws working for the governor. Besides, we both knew his rationale was sheer nonsense. He continued to babble about this and that, making it clear that what Jim had thought was true: I threatened this guy. The only way he could keep me down (and feel superior) was by denying me the title of mayor. I knew it and he knew it.

Before I hung up the phone, I told him: "I hope you're very proud of yourself and feel good about your decision. I hope that it was worth it and that you can sleep at night."

"I sure will be able to sleep tonight," he said with a trembling voice.

After that, I couldn't bring myself to ever talk with him for more than a few minutes at a time. I made sure to always act professionally when conducting city business with him, but our interactions were kept to a bare minimum. Sadly, where there had once been the "three musketeers" getting things done for our city, there was now a divided city council that did not often see eye to eye on issues. And then, sadly, my dear friend Raul passed away in October 1995. His loss was devastating. The entire council was altered. Where Latinos had once been the majority of the council, now I was the lone no vote. All the prior dreams we had for our city were crumbling. The person who filled Raul's seat was decided by the current mayor's third vote (I wasn't surprised). Some members of the council became more concerned with making deals for their friends than creating real change. As I witnessed this, somewhere in the back of my mind I heard my grandmother's words of wisdom: "There is no ill that lasts one hundred years and no sick man that can endure it." In other words, this too would pass.

And it did, but not before I would learn another valuable lesson. The time came when both the former and current mayors were seeking reelection. This time around, they were running against each other. Both of their messages boiled down to finger pointing at the other guy not being fit for reelection. It was time for endorsements and I—guided again by what was best for the city—chose, hesitantly, to endorse the man who had betrayed me. I resigned myself to choosing the lesser of two evils.

The response to my endorsement was disbelief. Many questioned why I would support someone who had wronged me; they felt that he did not deserve my support and that the best course of action would be for me to withhold it and prevent him from returning to the council. In my heart, however, I knew that the other guy's policies were no good either. If he were reelected, it would be because of the name recognition he had from being a longtime member of the council. In the end, my betrayer was reelected as was the mayor.

In retrospect, I should have been guided by the old saying that the lesser of two evils is still evil. Hindsight is 20/20 and, knowing what I know today, I would've stayed out of the race. At the time, I felt that he had learned from his mistakes—that if he had a chance to take it all back, he would.

During the next cycle of his reelection I did the same thing: I supported my betrayer's reelection. The dynamics of this campaign, however, were entirely different, as he was the only council member seeking reelection. The other council member (and former mayor) was wisely not seeking reelection because he knew that he would not be elected; he had made some controversial remarks that insulted the community of a city with dramatically shifting demographics.

Many members of the community—including members of the California legislature—interpreted his comments as racist and made calls for his resignation.

As I had done in the past, I went out of my way to ensure the success of the person I was supporting—in this case my betrayer once again. It had been the custom of the council that the mayor would serve two years in a row. It was now my turn to seek the mayorship for one more year. My betrayer decided, once again, not to vote for me. This time around, the pain and disappointment were absent. I was at complete peace with myself, secure in the knowledge that I had always placed the city's best interest before my pain or desire for vengeance. In my mind, he was a poor sour soul who couldn't help himself. There was no pity for him. I had learned my lesson: a man who betrays you once will certainly betray you twice.

The whole experience reminded me of the tale of the Indian boy who, in order to prove he has reached manhood, is charged with the task of collecting a handful of flowers that only grow at the top of a steep mountain. The boy— with hopes of soon being regarded as a man—knows that this is a task fraught with peril, but he will not disappoint the tribe's chief. The boy sets out with determination to the mountain's summit and, after several ordeals, finally collects the flowers. As he is preparing to descend, several feet away, he sees a snake that is writhing in pain. The snake begs the boy to please take him down the mountain so he can seek help. The boy initially refuses, saying, "You're a snake. One bite from you can kill me. I'm so close to becoming a man and can't take a chance like that." The snake continues to writhe painfully: "If you leave me here I will surely die. I promise you that although I am a snake, I will not bite you. Please have pity on me." The boy hesitates awhile longer and finally tells the snake to promise him one last time before he slips the snake into a pouch. The boy continues his trek down the mountain, excited to reach the tribal chief.

After several more hours, the boy finally reaches the foot of the mountain and sees the chief's content smile. The snake, sensing their journey is ending, asks to please be let out as she is having trouble breathing. The boy leans down to let the snake free. The snake immediately snaps her head and sinks her teeth deeply into the boy's arm.

"I don't understand. How could you do this to me after I brought you down this mountain? What about your promise?"

As the snake slithers away, she says, "When you picked me up, you knew I was a snake."

The lesson I learned: a snake would always be a snake.

Governor Wilson Comes to Huntington Park

On the state level, Governor Wilson was reelected and the much-contested Proposition 187 passed and sent a wave of devastation through the Hispanic community. Undocumented immigrants became scapegoats for a wide array of unrelated problems. Even though it was immediately challenged in court as unconstitutional, many Latino families stopped sending their children to school. Hospitals and doctors avoided taking patients unable to prove their legal status. The list of atrocities went on. Our community in Huntington Park was simmering with contempt, distrust, and anger. Although I had supported the governor's reelection, I was pained by the effects his Proposition 187 had on the community.

Although not related to the proposition's passing, the gang violence in Huntington Park spiraled out of control. The spark that made the situation blow up in the media occurred on Halloween night in 1995. A drive-by shooting took the life of a young Latina by the name of Erika Estrada while she sat on her front porch. Our city began making headlines for all the wrong reasons. I was always at the forefront of the city's fight against gangs, but it was clear that they were winning. At this time, the governor proposed legislation to deal with the crime but needed a location within California to launch the initiative that would implement civil injunctions against gang members. I knew what I needed to do. I invited the governor to our city in hopes that his arrival would highlight its plight and bring resources to our city.

My invitation prompted an immediate community response. On one side, many were tired of the gang violence and saw the governor's visit as possible help. And yet others, such as the Latino leadership and media, were in disbelief that I'd invited the man who had pushed for Proposition 187 to pass. Radio programs chastised me for inviting the "devil" to our city. During a radio interview, a host asked me point-blank if I was crazy for hosting the governor in our city. I answered her plainly: "I opposed Proposition 187 but whether we like it or not, it has been approved by the voters—until the courts decide otherwise. More important, however, is the fact that Proposition 187 has yet to kill anyone, while gangs continue to do so. If the governor is willing to come in and help us deal with this problem, then we should be grateful." The host grudgingly acknowledged my point, but she was still not on board. This was one of many conversations I'd have with the community explaining how we could be both against Proposition 187 and against gang violence.

Once the governor decided that, in Huntington Park, he would launch the crime initiative, I began to hear rumors that protestors were going to flock to the kickoff event. Calls came in suggesting I relinquish my invitation. I was distraught because I did not want Proposition 187's controversy to upstage the severe need to deal with our gang problem. Both were important issues, but the death of our community's children was a more immediate concern. Others, however, had a different opinion. I had one council member from a neighboring city walk into my office and demand that I listen to him.

"Listen, *mi'jita* [dear child], I really like you and think you have a promising future ahead of you," he said, wagging his finger at me, "but I'm telling you right here and right now and you better listen carefully. If you bring that *diablo* to where *la raza* is, your political career is over."

It took me a moment to regain my composure after this verbal assault.

"You know, you're absolutely right," I said. "If I was only concerned with my political career, I wouldn't invite him here or even take a photo with him."

"So you know what you must do," he said.

"Yes, I do," I said. "I must be the kind of councilwoman who does not put her political career ahead of children's lives."

"You have so much to learn," he said.

"That may be true, but if I fail to get reelected at the end of my term, at least I will know I did everything I could to make sure that our streets are safer."

"Well, you've been given notice," he said, and then walked out of my office.

I'm a firm believer that if you are true to your convictions and are honest with people about them, then you may even earn the respect of your enemies. As he exited my office, I hoped that even if he didn't agree with my actions, he'd learn I deserved his respect.

It took time, but slowly our community began to turn around. The police force was extensively trained and became known as the strongest in the area. There was an effective crackdown on gangs and *miqueros* (sellers of false documents) that was evident not only visually, but also in the crime rate statistics. There was a concerted effort to improve our schools and the air quality. If people didn't reelect me, that'd be fine because I could rest knowing I had done everything to protect them.

A couple of years later when I ran for reelection, everyone had already written my political obituary. There was no way as a Republican—especially one who worked for Governor Wilson—that I had a shot at remaining on the council. I became an easy target during the race, as the political numbers were not on my side: I was the only Republican running out of nine candidates. Huntington Park was also a city where Democrats outnumbered Republicans three to one. And yet, my community looked past party affiliations to the numbers that mattered: the crime rates were lower and the city was a safer place to live in. Not only was I reelected; I was now the mayor and the top vote-getter.

There were plenty of challenges in the seven years I served on city council. I learned that local politics could be as rewarding as they are challenging. I learned many valuable lessons that have served me until this day. Never did I think, however, that my efforts were being noticed miles away by the Republican governor of Texas.

10. Treasuring Opportunities

I was one of a handful of people invited by the Republican Party to greet George W. Bush—then the governor of Texas—at Hawthorne Airport. He was visiting California to officially announce his intention to seek the Republican nomination for the presidency. Our introduction was one I'd never forget:

"Governor, this is Rosario Marín, the mayor of the city of Huntington Park," a woman said.

"Oh, *el alcalde*!" Bush said.

I tried to hold back, but I couldn't help correcting his Spanish. "No, I think you mean *la alcaldeza,*" which is the proper term for a female mayor.

"Oh, *la alcaldeza,*" he repeated mockingly, not missing a beat. Everyone around us laughed.

We exchanged pleasantries and instantly clicked. He was disarming and easygoing in a way that made me feel as though we had been friends for years.

With time, I became convinced that George W. Bush would make a great president, especially for the Latino community. The way he interacted with Latinos was authentic, warm, and relaxed. It didn't come from media training, but from growing up in Texas, a state chock-full of colonias and barrios. It wasn't just about politics with him. After researching his positions on issues, I was sold.

I signed up to be a volunteer and surrogate for his campaign. I was acquainted with key California campaign players, and they knew of my political credentials from the time I worked for Governor Wilson. It wasn't long before I was invited to every presidential campaign event in California. I provided more interviews to the Latino media than any other surrogate across the nation and was soon known as the Latina spokesperson for the campaign. When the election results were being contested, I was the only nonlawyer Bush's campaign trusted to speak with the Latino media.

Looking back, it doesn't seem fathomable that I was able to have so many balls in the air at once. In addition to being a council member, I was working full-time as the public affairs manager for AT&T's Hispanic market in the Southern California region. And now, I had fallen into this new position of helping the Bush campaign. With the three-hour difference between the East and West Coasts, there were times when my phone rang at four A.M. with somebody from the campaign on the other end of the line. Then I'd need to be in a television studio for the eleven o'clock evening news, often getting home at midnight—all in a day's work. Throughout all of this, I tried to spend as many stolen moments as possible with my children. I explained to them that I was going through an intense work phase. It was important to me that I didn't shrink from these demands on my time because I knew that if Bush became president, there would be more attention given to the needs of the growing Latino community, especially schoolchildren.

This was the first time I became active on a national scale; I had no idea that people who work on presidential campaigns sometimes end up working for the administration. The only thing I cared about was which candidate would be the best for my community. It was a challenging heap of work, but it rarely feels like that when your heart and soul are in it.

In hindsight, I see that there were certain occurrences that foretold a potential place for me in the administration. Whether or not some of these events were coincidental, predestined, or perhaps both, I don't know. What I do know is that each occurrence brought me to a better understanding of the future president. One example is from the first time I was selected to greet him at the airport. The greeting line is a sort of hierarchal arrangement with the highest ranking (or most important) official being the first to greet the incoming guest, and so on. I was the ninth person out of ten. I always joke that I'm grateful there was somebody less important than I was. And yet, when he finished shaking hands with everyone, he stood right next to me and said: "Well, I guess they are waiting for us to start the press conference." At his side, I accompanied him to where the press conference was to take place. Where that first greeter/most important person was standing during the press conference I can't say. But I know that I was standing on Bush's right-hand side. If I had tried to engineer circumstances to turn out this way, it most likely wouldn't have happened.

On another occasion, in 2000, I attended the National Council of La Raza's annual conference in the San Diego Convention Center. NCLR is the largest national Latino civil rights and advocacy organization in the country, with thousands of people attending its conference every year. It was an important event for George W. Bush to attend as a presidential candidate. By the time he arrived to address the conference, I was already at the media stands ready to offer my reactions to reporters. My friend Leslie Sanchez was coordinating the Latino media's response to the campaign and was pacing around frantically. When she saw me, she asked that I please go downstairs to attend a small rally that was welcoming our candidate. I told her I was already in my place and, pointing down at my high-heeled shoes, explained that it was getting painful to walk around. She pleaded with me and I sensed that something had fallen by the wayside. She explained that there weren't a lot of people gathered because they were all attending the conference: "There are more cameras than people down there and the campaign wants more bodies in the audience." I finally relented and made it clear that she owed me one. On my way down, I saw a few friends and corralled them downstairs with me.

As we approached where the welcoming party was gathering, I noticed George P. Bush (the candidate's nephew) had just arrived. I called out "Jorge" in Spanish to get his attention. He turned around, flashed me a huge smile, and asked me to come with him. I had met him a couple of times during campaign events and he had always been such a gentleman. Just as we were stepping into place, the motorcade with the candidate arrived as if on cue. When George W. got out of the car, he spotted his nephew and called out, "Hey P., come over here." He waved for both of us to come over. I was the first person he greeted He shook my hand and with a smile said, "Great to see you again, *alcaldeza*." There were many photographers at the event and each of his movements sparked enough wattage to light an entire village.

When the next morning arrived, the last thing I expected was to be present in the campaign photo that appeared worldwide that day. To my astonishment, the same picture was also chosen to portray the Bush campaign in the 2001 *World Almanac*. All this, and I hadn't even planned on being at the rally. Again, I doubt anything like that would've occurred if I had sought to make it happen.

Then there was the time when Bush (already president-elect) invited a group of Latino leaders to Austin in order to develop an agenda for the community. I had been on a conference call with one of the participants, and before we got off he said that he looked forward to seeing me in Austin in two days. I told him I wasn't going to be in Austin because I hadn't received an invitation. He then shared with me that there must be some mistake because he had seen the list and my name was definitely on it. Once we were off the phone, I called my contact at the campaign and inquired about the situation. There was a pause, and then: "Oh my God, Rosario, I was supposed to call you and ask that you come, and it totally slipped my mind. Can you please make the trip?" I told her that I would try my best, but I'd have to cancel appointments and make travel arrangements. It was so close to Christmastime and I was busy with the normal seasonal activities. "Oh, please forgive me. I really hope you can make it, especially because I know my boss will be really upset if you don't. I'll be in so much trouble."

Luckily, I was able to make the trip. When I arrived, Christmastime had brought cold temperatures to Austin. At the meeting site, the leather seats were arranged in a U formation with accompanying name tags and two rows of seats in the back. Since I was one of the last to RSVP, I started my name tag search near the back of the room. One of the assistants asked my name and when I told him, he said, "Oh, ma'am, you're over here. I placed your name tag myself." I followed him. The first name tag I saw read: George W. Bush. Next to his I saw my own name tag.

The assistant smiled when he saw my disbelief. How was this possible? Whom did I have to thank? I know people in politics go through all kinds of shenanigans to be seated in coveted places. To this day, I don't know who (if anyone) arranged that seat for me. Some people are convinced that was the day the soon-to-be president decided I should be asked to be the next treasurer.

The meeting got started and eventually it was my turn to speak. I started calmly but soon found myself in a passionate discourse about the dire situation of Latino students. Something needed to be done—and soon! I don't remember the specific words I used, but I do remember Bush's paying close attention to what I was saying. When I was through he thanked me, and before calling on the next speaker, turned to me and said: "Don't ever lose that passion."

Election day came, and with it passed the five wrenching weeks when the nation didn't know who the next president would be. After the Supreme Court made its ruling, my husband and I were invited to the inauguration.

Most of our memories of Washington weren't so pleasant, as they revolved around visiting Eric's doctor when he was having the spasms. Now, however, the day I had been looking forward to since the beginning of the campaign was here. It was special for me because in my own small way I felt I had contributed to the president-elect's success. As I saw him being sworn in by the chief justice of the United States, I felt humbled: here I was, an immigrant to this country, watching history unfold right before my eyes.

After all the celebrations, I returned to California, happy and ready to get back to business. On my return, I was taken aback when people asked me which position in the administration I was going after. As far as I was concerned, I was content with the role I had played in the election and now considered my job done. I was focused on catching up on work in both the city council and my position with AT&T. True to my nature, I just headed back to work.

Then came the phone call.

On the other end of the line a woman identified herself as a member of the presidential personnel. Then she asked me a question I'll never forget: "Ms. Marín, would you be willing to be considered for the position of treasurer of the United States?" I flipped through my calendar—it wasn't April Fool's Day. My chin was on the floor and I tried desperately to pick it up in order to answer the voice on the other end of the line. I tried, unsuccessfully, to sound coherent, but mostly I made a series of garbled sounds that could never pass for words. I didn't know exactly what the treasurer did, but if I was deemed fit for the job, then who was I to argue? I was finally able to compose myself.

"I am so honored that you called me," I said. "As a matter of fact, if you never call me back, you've already made my day, my year, my life."

She chuckled.

"I'm usually pretty eloquent," I said, taking a deep breath, "but right now I'm downright speechless. You're probably questioning my mental health."

"Ms. Marín, it's quite all right. I understand the effect a phone call like this can have on someone."

She began to ask me a few questions and suggested that the process could be intimidating. "If there is anything you've done wrong, now's the time to come clean because they'll find out about it in no time."

"No problem," I replied. "I've gone through two political campaigns and have been under close scrutiny. Believe me, my political opponents would've dug up any dirt by now."

She told me that this process would be even more thorough: it would include extensive background checks as well as a review of my finances. My entire life would come under microscopic scrutiny.

"I have no reservations at all," I said.

"Then, good. I just ask that you keep this call confidential. You can tell your husband and children, but no one else. And no exceptions."

I hung up the phone and started to pace, and then paced some more, entering an absorbing daze. I went up and down the stairs, over and over. My children were at school and my husband was at work. I was home alone and didn't even know where to begin unraveling the questions. I was too excited to think everything through. What a wonderful opportunity and unexpected challenge. What if I actually did become treasurer of the United States? It would be such a gift. What made it all the better was that I had not even sought the position. Yes, I had worked on the campaign, but so had thousands of others. Was it possible that this, too, was meant to be? I thought back to all of the coincidences throughout the campaign and it all seemed to come together.

Unlike other people, who knew exactly which position they would ask for if their candidate won, I didn't even want to move to Washington. I had worked on the campaign with no expectation of anything in return—I just knew that George W. would be a great president. Now I know that one of the reasons I was offered the position is precisely because I had made no demands. According to my fried Raul Romero—the point person on the campaign for Latino issues—the president chose me because of my accomplishments and personal story. He said that the president liked people who had rough beginnings and were not pretentious, but humble. The fact that I had not demanded anything only proved that there was no expectation of quid pro quo.

Eventually my pacing stopped—it had to. I called my husband at work and practically cut him off before he could finish saying hello. I told him of the phone call from the White House and how I had been caught so off guard that I had just agreed to be considered for the position of treasurer of the United States. My husband, as I had been at first when the call came, was speechless. Then he snowed me with an avalanche of questions I couldn't keep up with. The next time I was on the phone with the White House, I told him, I'd be sure to get some answers. That was, of course, if they ever called me back, considering how giddy and inarticulate I had been.

My husband laughed, saying that he was sure they'd call me back. "I'm very proud of you," he said. "We're going to have a long discussion when I get home." I agreed; just considering all the changes sent my mind reeling.

In the meantime, I made sure to keep mum, and not tell my brothers, sisters, and mom about the big news. Alex and I discussed the phone call with our three children, making them promise not to tell anyone, not even their best friends. We felt that it was important to let our children know as soon as possible about the potential sacrifices that becoming treasurer would entail. At the end of our conversation, Carmen—only twelve—reminded me of our family motto: "To whom much is given, much is expected." I thanked her for reminding me and decided that we would take this one step at a time.

I spent many long hours thinking about what all this would mean. Similar to when I had been appointed to serve in Governor Wilson's administration, my family would have to start a new life. This time, however, it would be three thousand miles away from our home, as opposed to only four hundred. We would have to sell our house in Huntington Park to be able to afford a new one in D.C. The children would be uprooted just the way I was when I was around their age and came to the United States.

How quickly time passed.

We often had impromptu family gatherings. A move

would mean the familial support system that we enjoyed so much (and relied on) would no longer be there. Our parents were also getting older, and the thought that we wouldn't be around in the case of an emergency weighed heavily on me. In the past I had sought advice for such ground-shifting career moves, but now I could not.

Although it was difficult, I kept to my routine. No one had a clue about what I was going through. When people suggested I deserved an appointment within the administration, I would shrug and say that it wasn't up to me. In the meantime, the appointing process was moving forward smoothly. I had a series of interviews and the extensive background checks continued. It was nearly a month before I found out that the White House would soon make the announcement. I was finally allowed to tell my family. It was important for me to tell my mother before the official announcement as she had a heart problem. I visited her home and chatted for a while before I told her that the president was going to announce my nomination as the next treasurer of the United States.

"Isn't that a very high position?" she asked innocently.

"Oh yes, Mom. It's huge!"

"Wouldn't it be better if he started you out with something a little smaller? Wouldn't it be too much work?"

This made me laugh. "Well, Mom, if the president thinks I can do it, then I must be able to do it."

"I just worry about you, honey," she said.

"I know, Mom, but I'll be fine," I said.

As a mother, I understood where she was coming from. It wasn't that she didn't think I was capable, but rather that she was concerned about my well-being, about the toll such a position could take on me and my family. I would be making such a giant leap in my career and she wouldn't be there in case I fell. Here I was, a fully grown woman being considered for a distinguished position in the administration, and my mom could only see me as her little girl.

The day the announcement was made, my entire family had gone camping. I had to stay behind because I had council duties to attend to. My husband, in recounting the day, said that my brothers wanted him to drink a lot of champagne in hopes of having him agree to change my name back to my maiden name or at least hyphenate my current name. They knew with my new position came the honor of having my signature on every U.S. bill. Alex said no amount of champagne was going to be enough for him to agree to that. I adopted my husband's last name when we got married, and for the past twenty years everyone knew me as Rosario Marín, not Rosario Spíndola. I cannot blame my brothers. They explained that nobody would believe that their sister was the treasurer of the United States, but if I had the same last name, it would aid them in their glorious bragging.

The well wishes of friends and acquaintances came pouring in—and from so many places. With pile after pile of flower arrangements arriving at all hours, my living room looked like either a funeral home or flower shop. There were so many that I had no choice but to start giving them out to family members.

My community was proud of me and I knew that I acted as a reflection of them—they could see themselves in me. I was moved to tears time and time again when young and old, rich and poor, told me how proud they were of me. I was determined to make good on that pride.

One particular memory has stayed with me. A few days after the announcement, I was eating in El Ranchito, a local restaurant, where a woman selling flowers was making her way around the restaurant. The restaurant manager purchased a bouquet and brought the woman over to my table.

"I just wanted to let you know that this lovely bouquet is going to the next treasurer of the United States," the manager said.

With the entire restaurant now turned toward us, I couldn't help but blush.

"Oh, I heard about her on the news," she said. "She's just like me, from Huntington Park."

I shook hands with her; she looked radiant.

"Wow, a Latina like me. You make me so proud," she said.

It was then that I realized how important my being the first immigrant treasurer would be for my community.

The next few weeks presented an interesting dilemma for me: presidential nominees are not allowed to give any interviews about their appointments. This proved difficult because up until that point I was constantly in the media as a spokesperson for Governor Wilson, as a council member, as a mayor, and then as a representative of the Bush campaign. Oddly, now that this was directly about me, I wasn't allowed to speak with reporters. The Latino media hounded me and the White House agreed that I could issue a statement, but that was it. No interviews or any other contact; I had to limit my comments to the prepared statement. I understood the media's persistence; the story of an immigrant's becoming treasurer of the United States was headline news for both the Latino and immigrant communities.

Of course, I didn't have time to focus on the historical import of what was happening—I needed to prepare for the confirmation hearing. While the White House was confident of my confirmation, I was still prepped thoroughly for the hearings. I asked whether I needed to get letters of support, but I was reassured that there were no indications that any senator had a problem with my appointment. My husband would be the only person from my family who would accompany me to the confirmation hearing.

He joined me in Washington the night before and we slept in my dear friend Ana Maria Farias's bedroom. She insisted on giving up her room for the night because she said I needed a good night's sleep. Little did she know that no matter how comfortable I was, I barely slept a wink. I don't think anyone facing a U.S. Senate confirmation can sleep. I rehearsed my answers to questions that had been presented to me time and time again. I made up new, more challenging questions and answered those, too. In the end I'm sure fatigue eventually gave way to sleep.

When we arrived at the Dirksen Senate Office Building the next morning, I was overwhelmed with excitement. It was a humbling experience to be a part of this historic day for the immigrant community. There were six appointees up for confirmation that day and most only had their spouses or a couple of their children with them. In addition to my husband, I wanted to share such a momentous day with some of my closest friends: Ana Maria Farias, Leslie Sanchez, Theresa Alvillar Speake, Adrianne Cisneros, and Shirley Wheat (my right-hand woman). A couple of people from the Treasury were also there to hear my prepared statement.

It was a short statement that declared my intent while outlining my life's story and professional background. As I read it, all my rehearsing went out the window as I expressed how honored I was at the moment to even be considered. I had never imagined all those years ago when I arrived on U.S. soil that I'd be there in front of the Senate. When I was done reading the statement, there was absolute silence. I was later told that some people in the audience had tears in their eyes. Senator Max Baucus and Senator Orrin Hatch offered kind comments. There were no questions for me—and I was relieved. Once the hearing was over I was bombarded by warm hugs and kisses. I remember leaving the room, entering a new bout of disbelief that I was now that much closer to becoming the forty-first treasurer of the United States.

The question did remain as to whether the Senate was going to take up my confirmation before the senators left for their August recess. It looked as though it may only occur after they returned, so I planned to return to California by the end of the week. Unlike other positions in the administration, the treasurer cannot be hired on an acting capacity, but can only begin service once being officially confirmed by the Senate. I resigned myself to not knowing the outcome until the Senate returned. I was scheduled to fly out of Washington on Friday afternoon—the last day the Senate was meeting. Just as I was about to leave the Senate Building that afternoon to catch my flight, Amy Best from Legislative Affairs rushed to tell me that the Senate had just voted unanimously to confirm me. Just like that, it was done.

I was ecstatic. I was virtually the treasurer of the United States. She explained that the only thing left was for the president to sign my commission papers and then it would be official. She said that he was already in Crawford, Texas, for his summer working vacation, but that my papers would land on his desk first thing, in next week's signature file.

I let my family know immediately. Although they knew that this would mean changes were afoot, they were elated when I returned to Los Angeles. My forty-third birthday would be the next day and the Senate had given me the best gift I could've asked for. On Sunday, as usual, we went to church. We had a lot to be grateful for and to celebrate. The parishioners were in a festive mood, and many congratulated us. The next step was to make all the arrangements for my entire family to join me for the swearing-in ceremony. My husband, children, mom, dad, brothers, sisters, and best friends would all surround me on this momentous day. Flori—the woman who has helped take care of my children since Alex was less than a year old—would also be there. Without the peace of mind that she granted me when I was away, I don't think I would have been able to accomplish so much. The final head count was thirty-six, all flying from California to D.C. to witness one of the most important days of my life.

When August 16, 2001, the day of my of swearing-in, arrived, I was awestruck as I walked into the press room with Secretary Paul O'Neill, who was ready to administer the oath of office. He was surprised by the great number of cameras: every Latino news outlet was present to record swearing in of the first immigrant to be given the honor of becoming treasurer of the United States. My children were beside me and Alex was holding the Bible. I looked to the front row and although there were other people I knew there, all I saw were my mom and dad as though a spotlight was encircling them. Tears made their way down my dad's face and my mom radiated pride.

I could only imagine what was running through their minds at that moment. Their decision to bring us to the United States was bearing great fruit. I knew that they were proud of me, but they also had a deep appreciation for this nation that had given their child unimaginable opportunities. My appointment exceeded the American Dream my parents had hoped their children would attain. Reciting the oath in that sea of emotions was surreal. *This is for them,* I thought. After all, without the two gifts they had given me of a strong work ethic and faith, I would not be standing there. I knew then that I'd never be able to fully repay them, but I hoped that this was at least a good down payment for their immeasurable sacrifices.

Getting Down to Business

As the U.S. treasurer, I now had unprecedented opportunities to work in areas that could have a great impact on the lives of the less fortunate. In addition to my regular duties of overseeing the production of currency, I led financial literacy efforts to decrease the number of "unbanked." This group consists of ten million people—mainly poor Americans and newly arrived immigrants. I was fundamental in expanding the market for remittances (money that people working in the U.S. send to Mexico and other countries). I also counted myself a member of the president's economic team that was charged with the duty of selling his economic packages. Last, but certainly not least, I served on the White House Initiative on Educational Excellence for Hispanic Americans. In other words, I had a lot of work ahead of me.

Giving My John Hancock

Soon enough, Secretary O'Neill and I went to the Bureau of Engraving and Printing (located near the Treasury) to see the first sheets of dollar bills with our signatures on them fly off the printing press. Once again, an army of photographers was in attendance.

With each sheet the press ejected, the reality of what was occurring became more concrete. A few days later, the bureau allowed me to pay for a few dollar bills with my signature on them. It would be a while before the bills with my signature would be in circulation, but I had my own supply early. I held the stack of crisp bills and couldn't wait to show them to my family.

The next time I saw my little sister Nancy, I told her I had something to show her. I took a dollar bill complete with signature from my wallet. When she saw my name, we joined hands and began to jump up and down. It wasn't until then, as I giggled and bounced, that I realized how much I had been suppressing my emotions. Obviously it wouldn't have been a good career move to jump up and down when all the cameras were on me. But in privacy with my sister I was free to have the unencumbered outburst of a child.

I wondered if Michael Hillegas—the first U.S. treasurer—also experienced the same thrill at seeing his signature on the currency. I was taking my place in history as the forty-first treasurer, and even now when I think about how privileged few have had this honor, it still fills me with a deep sense of awe and gratitude. To think that many years from now, my name will still be in somebody's hand or behind a museum case is mind-boggling.

9/11

On the morning of September 11, 2001, I awoke to begin again my new routine as treasurer. It had not even been a month since my swearing-in ceremony.

Although I rarely watch television in the mornings, for some reason I had on *Good Morning America* as I got ready for work in my friend's condo in Virginia. My family had yet to relocate to D.C. but I had already started my position. I was just about to head over to the Treasury when Diane Sawyer interrupted the program with the announcement that there had been an accident in one of the Twin Towers in New York—they were trying to get a live shot of it. As I sat down, eyes glued to the screen, I saw a second plane crash into the second tower. I remember Sawyer's next comment being something to the effect of, "Did everybody see what I think I saw? Could we replay that?"

I dialed my husband in California. When he answered, I knew that I had awoken him.

"Alex, we're at war," I said, surprised at my own words. I somehow knew in my heart that those two strikes couldn't be an accident.

"What are you talking about?"

"Just turn on the television," I said, knowing that the images would speak for themselves.

I heard the television turn on and immediately wished I were back in California with my children.

"Oh my God," he said.

"I know," I said. "Please tell the children when they wake up that we are engaged in war."

"Okay. Take care of yourself, Rosario."

"I will and I'll be home as soon as possible," I said, and then I hung up.

For some reason, I was certain that the attack would mean war. I certainly had no knowledge of threats to our country, but it was clear to me that this was different from the wars the United States had fought before.

I decided to head to the Treasury. *How can the sky be such a gorgeous blue when something like this is happening?* I thought as I exited the house. Just as I was reaching for the car door handle, I heard a distant and awful sound behind me. Where I was staying was close to the Pentagon and when I turned around I saw a monstrous cloud of black smoke billowing up into the air. My heart began to thump. I fumbled for the car keys and got in. I pulled onto the George Washington Parkway in the direction of Reagan National Airport. The smoke was getting closer. I passed the airport and then to the left I saw a sight I will never forget: the Pentagon was in flames.

My body went into shock. My cell phone vibrated; it was my friend Ana Maria in Texas. We said hello and immediately lost reception.

By the time I crossed the 14th Street Bridge, pandemonium had descended. Cars were surfacing from parking garages as others trying to make their way in were turned away. I was unsuccessful in reaching the Treasury Building parking lot. The Secret Service had locked down the White House compound, which included the Treasury. Some people were walking out of buildings while others were running. It was a state of confusion that soon led to gridlock. I couldn't get in touch with any of my staff and was unable to park anywhere. Defeated, I turned around and headed back to my friend's condo.

The thought that the Treasury Building, White House, or even the Capitol could be hit next was frightening. After all, these hits were no coincidence. I wondered whether I'd be able to return to my family in California anytime soon, or ever. On the way back to the condo, I bought some water and emergency supplies. Like many, I was glued to the television. I peeled myself away the next day long enough to venture into D.C. It was a ghost town. If it weren't for the police personnel guarding the buildings, I'd have thought I was the last person on earth. Gone was the vibrant and energetic city; what was left was a city draped in black. More than scared, I was deeply saddened. The wound that had been inflicted at the heart of this nation was painfully obvious. Armed guards patrolled the streets. For a second I felt as though I were in a third world country. This just wasn't the way it was supposed to be, especially not in the nation's capital.

A few days later, we were able to return to work. I was proud of the vast majority of federal employees who went back to work. It was clear that intimidation by any means would not prevent us from doing our duty. I made sure to visit and shake hands with the workers at the Bureau of Engraving and Printing. I thanked them for their willingness to do their duty in spite of the fears or reservations they might have had. As a site essential to the functioning of our economy, they were a natural target. The employees' commitment in light of events heartened me. I was proud to lead such a committed workforce.

One man in particular said that he knew he had to do his job, and by the same token he expected everyone else to do theirs. Looking around, I knew that this was the best way to get back at the terrorists: we were not going to bow to them. We were proud Americans and there was no doubt that we'd pull through.

I visited New York City a week after the tragedy. My friend Ana Maria Farias from the Housing and Urban Development Department made arrangements for me to talk to the people working in HUD's New York office. The stories they shared of witnessing people jumping from the burning towers were horrendous. The New York police escorted me to the area where the buildings had collapsed. I could almost hear the collective screaming of the thousands who'd tried to escape the area. My heart ached imagining the utter desperation of parents who knew they'd never see their children again, and vice versa. Words failed anyone trying to articulate the scale of the devastation. Nothing I could write could do it justice.

Of course there were a lot of questions about how safe we were as a nation. 9/11 changed everything. All of a sudden we felt vulnerable. We realized we *were* vulnerable. If the terrorists hit us once, they could certainly do it again. The only question seemed to be when and where. The airports reopened five days later, and I was scheduled to fly back to California the following day. I had already made the arrangements before the tragedy because the city of Huntington Park was going to host a reception in my honor. Also, the following day I was to celebrate my twentieth wedding anniversary.

When I arrived at Dulles International Airport, it was eerily empty. There were a handful of people clustered here and there, but none of the typical hustle and bustle. For once I wouldn't have minded waiting in a long line to get to the ticket counter. The people who were ready to board looked at one another with varying levels of distrust. No one engaged anyone else in conversation. There was a general feeling of everyone being on the edge. No more than ten people boarded the plane coming back to Los Angeles. Although the airline staff must have been just as jittery as we were to board the planes, they did—making a bold statement that we weren't going to have our lives ruled by terror. I prayed while the plane taxied on the runway. I'm sure I wasn't the only one who imagined our flight having a similar fate. The whole experience was nerve-racking. It felt as though we were collectively holding our breath. When the plane's back wheels touched down on the L.A. runway, I exhaled and released my tears.

Thank God, I was going to be able to see my family again.

Today, I sometimes can't help but get impatient when people cannot understand what we had to endure individually and collectively. For so many people in New York, D.C., and the entire country, life would never be the same. We have been tested in more ways than we ever wanted to be. My family was alive and well, and yet the thought that I might never see them again haunted me. This felt like a very different kind of war because it had touched down on our soil; it was not something that was happening "somewhere over there." I knew that the Treasury Building could be the next target. The more visible police presence served as a deterrent, but also it was a sad reminder that we weren't as safe as we had once thought. Many of our daily routines were altered when the security of our nation became the top priority. The economic impacts of the attacks were felt worldwide. It became clear, however, that the foundation of our economy was strong enough to avoid sliding into a depression, as some feared.

A few weeks after the attacks, I took a trip to where the gold reserve is stored in Fort Knox. I wanted to send the message that all would be okay. Although our economy would suffer, the reserves were intact and ready to use if it should ever come to that. Not that such a thing would ever be necessary, but some felt comfortable knowing that I had toured the inner sanctum of our nation's gold reserve.

I made it a point to not only travel often after 9/11, but to fly on United and American Airlines—the same airlines that the terrorists had used in their attacks. I was doing my part to convey a sense of security to the public. Economically, the airline industry took the harshest hit with the attacks; in a small way, I wanted to contribute to their recovery. I know that many people had second and third thoughts about flying those specific airlines, but I didn't. The way I saw it, they were without fault and victims like so many others.

There was no doubt that our economy took a hit. The pillars that formed the foundation of our economy would ensure, however, that there would be an eventual recovery. There was an incredible amount of pressure placed on the president and the administration to deal with the economic fallout from the attacks. I was chosen to be a member of the team charged with the task of spreading the president's economic programs. I felt privileged to travel around the country to seek and secure support for the president's policies. I had the credibility to talk to bankers, businesspeople, and others about how the policies would turn the economy around. The president had already inherited an economy going into a recession and the attacks only worsened the already frail state of things. We needed to put money into people's pockets to avert another recession, and tax cuts would do the bulk of the work.

For the two years I was treasurer, I visited chambers of commerce, local businesses, newspapers, radio stations, and television stations. In time, we managed to convince many skeptical people who had originally questioned the validity of tax cuts to invigorate the economy. I firmly believe that had it not been for these precise cuts, our economy could've collapsed.

For our work on this team, the treasury secretary gave us an elegantly framed plaque of recognition. Although I was proud, no award could compare to seeing the economy well on its way to recovery.

My Speech to the Nation

As treasurer, it was my honor to travel the country and speak with the many affected by 9/11. What follows is an excerpt from a speech I wrote. It not only served to articulate what I felt, but also reminded our citizens that they are our country's most valuable treasure.

The aggressors may have taken thousands of lives but they have failed to rob us of our respect for life. Their fires may have burned down our buildings but the flames of our faith burn higher than their hatred. Our faith burns brighter than tyranny. The explosions may have shattered windows but the American spirit can never be broken. Buildings made of steel and cement were destroyed but the pillars of our society are stronger than steel and more solid than rock.

More than printing money, the United States has imprinted in every American the principles of freedom and opportunity. The United States, more than minting coins, has cast in every American the belief in liberty and the pursuit of happiness. No tyrant, no aggressor can ever make a dent in our beliefs. In our heritage and our legacy. As Treasurer of the United States, I have realized the true treasure of America, its people.

Financial ABCs

When I learned that there were ten million people in the United States who had never set foot inside a bank, it was clear that something needed to be done. As treasurer, I was in a unique position to help people become part of the financial system. My seven years of banking experience coupled with my background in local government gave me a firm understanding of the dynamics of why people do not participate in the system. On a personal level, I saw how intimidated my own parents were by banking institutions—so much so that they never opened a bank account in the U.S.

The magnitude of the educational effort that would be necessary to decrease the number of "unbanked" like my parents was significant. I felt strongly about helping those who suffered financial abuse due to their lack of banking knowledge and, sadly, their inability to understand English. I promised myself I would bring special attention to this segment of the population. My Spanish fluency made it possible to reach out to the Latino media and push for coverage about this social problem.

I worked with government, nonprofits, and the banking industry to increase financial literacy. Working with the financial services division, my office put together the first meeting among the Treasury Department, Department of Education, and many other stakeholders in the banking and financial industries. Together we designed a curriculum that hoped to seamlessly infuse current subjects already taught in schools with the basics of financial literacy. If we had decided to treat it as a separate subject there may have been more objections. I couldn't believe that there had never been a meeting between these two major departments to discuss issues that could have such a wide-ranging impact on the lives of so many.

It was alarming to learn that most students graduating from high school were not equipped with the financial tools to succeed. In many cases this meant that no matter how hard they worked, they would still be unsuccessful. This was not an issue exclusive to the poor and low-income population. It came as no surprise that the percentage of bankruptcies filed by those between the ages of eighteen and twenty-five had doubled in the last decade. If our young people didn't even understand the basic concept of compound interest, they probably wouldn't understand that paying only the minimum amount on their credit card bills could often translate into years of toil to get rid of even the smallest debt. Clearly, if graduating high school students lacked that kind of information, what could we expect of undereducated people who did not even speak English?

Within the Hispanic community, for instance, many banks and credit unions began a concerted effort to bring people into their institutions by partnering with local organizations to deliver programs. I tried to make a dent in this growing problem by highlighting the issues. Like many noble endeavors, this one must continue.

A Labor of Love

About a month after the 9/11 attacks, President Bush signed an executive order that created the White House Initiative on Educational Excellence for Hispanic Americans. Although it would've been understandable to cancel the signing ceremony because of what our country had just been through, Bush chose not to. This decision was telling of the high priority that the president placed on the serious educational challenges in the Latino community.

I was honored to be appointed the point person within the Treasury to serve on the commission. Our goal was to develop specific recommendations to increase the number of Latinos graduating from high school and, more important, enrolling in and completing a college education. The number of Latinos graduating from four-year universities was at an alarming low and the need for such a national initiative was long overdue. I traveled to a number of states to speak directly to children and schools. The executive director of the commission—my friend Leslie Sanchez—developed the first bilingual Web page to encourage Latino parents and students to attend college.

No matter where I traveled on behalf of the commission, I wore my heart on my sleeve. How could I not? I saw my own family in the faces that populated these depressed communities. In my own small way, I tried to give them hope by sharing my story. After my presentations, I'd often see mothers in tears, signs of their strong desire to see their children have a brighter future.

Of course, I knew on a personal level that a solid education could make all the difference. I'm almost certain that I would not have been appointed treasurer without my degree. I also saw the effects an education could have on an entire community. The city of Huntington Park had a 67 percent drop out rate, and as a result an underclass remained a permanent fixture of the community. I could speak from experience about what it meant to come from a community that didn't expect much from its children. President Bush recognized this when he would speak of the soft bigotry of low expectations. He was right: as a community we could no longer afford to lose so many of our young people to poor performance. And, more important, I could talk about what would be required of our community to reach common goals.

It was a labor of love for the commissioners, the product of which was a long report with specific recommendations. It's my hope that as our suggestions are implemented, more Latinos will graduate from college.

Rosario, the Ambassador

As the first Mexican-born treasurer, I made it a point to dive right into Mexico-related issues as soon as I came into office.

President Vicente Fox of Mexico and President Bush agreed that a prosperous Mexico would be in the best interest of both countries. It was agreed that a partnership would be formed and named the Partnership for Prosperity. The United States Treasury was the lead agency in this effort.

The official agreement would be made over a state dinner. I distinctively remember the night of the dinner. It was time to see fireworks from the White House balcony. The two presidential couples were standing together and I walked in to shake their hands.

President Bush immediately introduced me to President Fox: "*Señor Presidente, le presento a la Tesorera de los Estados Unidos,* Rosario Marín."

President Fox turned to shake my hand. "I've heard so much about you," he said. "What a pleasure it is to finally meet you. You've made us very proud."

There are no words I could use to fully capture that moment. Here was the president of the United States introducing me in Spanish and the president of Mexico greeting me in English!

With the fireworks blasting into the sky, I felt proud to be the highest-ranking Mexican-born woman in the Bush administration. I would be integral to this environment of friendship and camaraderie. The Partnership for Prosperity would give me the opportunity to work closely with high-level Mexican government officials to further common goals. In the process, I made strong friendships that will last a lifetime. I traveled to Mexico nine times in my two years as treasurer. I was extensively involved in promoting new services and products that made the best use of remittances—money sent from the U.S. to Mexico.

With my friend Mario Laborin—the head of NAFINSA, the Mexican equivalent of the Small Business Administration—we brought attention to Mexican women who could become entrepreneurs by opening businesses with the remittances received from their husbands in the United States. We promoted how people in the U.S. could buy construction materials in California and have them delivered directly to Mexico to build their dream houses. We knew that all these efforts could potentially help people realize their dreams while reducing the flow of undocumented immigrants into the U.S.

It was rewarding on so many levels to work with the two countries that made me who I am. The Mexican ambassador to the United States once told me that he considered me their third ambassador: "There's the U.S. ambassador, the Mexican ambassador, then there's Rosario the ambassador." I was honored that he would even suggest that, and I hoped I could fulfill that role.

An Issue That Hits Home

One of the most significant problems that needed to be tackled was putting an end to the abuse that those sending money back to Mexico were subjected to. Again, this was a mix of the personal with the professional for me.

Although it was more than thirty years in the past, the image of my mother desperately waiting for letters from my father with checks enclosed had made an indelible impression on me. Back then, Fridays were a day filled with an almost palpable tension as my mom waited outside our door for the postman to arrive. She would only come back inside after the delivery. We knew when it had arrived on time because she'd come back in adorned with an ear-to-ear smile. Often, however, she'd return with an air of defeat: "No luck today. Maybe on Monday." She worried constantly about how she was going to be able to feed us.

The business of remittances had grown exponentially over the last few years; more money was flowing into Mexico than ever before. Today, remittances make up the second largest source of income for Mexico, with petroleum exports taking first. The main problem was the concentration of power in the hands of the businesses sending money to Mexico. As no financial institutions were involved, there were no set standards. I was outraged to see the abuse that poor, uneducated, and hard-working people were facing—in some cases paying a 20 percent surcharge on the money they were sending to their families. I had personally seen the devastating effects these scams could wreak on families. As treasurer, I felt it was my duty to shed light on this issue.

This was a huge market and I strongly believe in the laws of supply and demand. While I don't believe in overregulating the marketplace, government intervention is necessary when market abuses undermine the greater good. There was simply no way to justify why people with no other recourse should have to pay so severely for such a simple transaction.

I followed the banking industry and knew that many banks were looking to expand their services. Wells Fargo decided to be the first to offer the service of remittances, and with that a domino effect began. Bank of America followed shortly after, and then Citicorp. Credit unions also wanted a piece of the pie, and in no time the entire banking industry was involved. The competition for this service was so stiff that the cost per transaction dropped dramatically—so rapidly that Bank of America began to offer the service for free. This had the wonderful outcome of greeting thousands into the financial system.

After serving two years as the treasurer, the opportunity to run for the United States Senate became a possibility. To think that I could make history again by becoming the first Latina to serve on the U.S. Senate—and have the opportunity to continue my life's mission—led me to resign from the best position I had ever held. I did it in spite of the potential risk it entailed. There was no guarantee that I would win the primary, much less the general election, against an incumbent senator. But as my grandmother used to say: *"El que no apuesta, no gana."* In other words, "One who risks nothing, wins nothing." Despite the odds, I felt the sacrifice was well worth it in order to accomplish a greater goal. The calling to a higher public office was undeniable.

11. The Chance of a Lifetime

I had been working at the Treasury for over a year and a half when one morning, as I was settling into my office chair, something caught my eye. To my left was a cup of coffee and to the right was *Roll Call,* a political newspaper that has been covering Capitol Hill since 1955. I cracked open the paper and spotted a full-page article about who would take on Barbara Boxer—the junior senator from California—during the next election cycle. Being from California, this article naturally piqued my interest. Eight people were mentioned, accompanied by pictures placed on a map of California. I stopped breathing for a second when I saw a picture of myself staring up at me from the page. I continued to read. The article said that GOP political consultants were suggesting my name.

I immediately went to talk to Michelle, the public affairs person at the Treasury. I was in panic mode because I worried that my position as treasurer could be compromised.

"Hi Michelle, I'm a bit concerned," I said. "There's this

article in *Roll Call* that I have nothing to do with. I'm not interested in a Senate position."

"Don't worry, Rosario, this is just typical Washington," she said, sensing my distress. "They like to speculate all the time."

I naively hoped that no one else would come across the article. No such luck. The calls came flooding in. It was a media storm that began in D.C. with calls from my friends and continued with calls from California. I won't say that I wasn't flattered by the suggestion that I would make a good senator. Of more concern, however, was doing the best I could within my current position.

Soon, I was swept up in the frenzy. Why would political consultants be throwing my name around? For that matter, who were these consultants? I still wasn't interested, but I was intrigued. I shared the article with my husband and we both decided to simply forget about the whole ordeal. My good friend Leslie Sanchez, however, became excited about the idea. She said that her political instincts pointed to potential in exploring the option. She articulated the many reasons it would make sense for me to pursue such an opportunity.

Although I believed that running for the Senate was something I was not ready to take on, a little question mark did erupt within my head: Could this be my next step? I promised myself to dismiss the whole idea and continue to concentrate on my job at the Treasury. Besides, since Eric was born I had stopped diligently planning out my future. It always seemed a lot more rewarding to focus on the task at hand. Time and again, I have reminded myself that I only have the present—I only have today.

September 1959. I am a little over one year old.

August 1973. My Quinceañera.

September 19, 1981. Alex and I at our wedding.

1985. I am expecting Eric.

September 1989. It's our anniversary and I am expecting Carmen.

1991. Eric and I when he is six years old.

1991. The family is complete! Alex W. has just been born (and is on my lap).

1995. My family and I at the Rose Fitzgerald Kennedy prize ceremony. Eunice Kennedy Shriver is standing to the left of me (*center*).

1998. All dressed up for Halloween.

January 2001. Alex and I at President George W. Bush's first inauguration.

August 2001. I am being sworn in by Secretary Paul O'Neill as the Treasurer of the United States.

August 2001. Friends and family from California join me in Washington, D.C., for my swearing in.

2001. Ceremony of the first dollars being released with my signature on them.
I am pictured with Secretary Paul O'Neill.

March 2002. My family and I visit Vicente Fox, President of Mexico, in Los Pinos.

July 2003. Pictured with my family, President Bush bids me farewell at the end of my time as U.S. Treasurer.

Nevertheless, I do keep my eyes and ears open in the present and, should an opportunity arise, why shouldn't I embrace it and run with it? Over the next few days, more questions took hold: Would it be foolish to pass up this opportunity? Was this a false hope? Or, simply: Was this the universe giving me a test?

The phone calls increased and more articles appeared in Washington and California. More and more reporters called the office requesting interviews with the "potential candidate." My staff politely dismissed the calls. I granted some interviews under the condition that questions in regard to the Senate run not be asked. I was doing my best to avoid seriously thinking about the possibility, but it was a futile effort. Even if my brain wouldn't engage in the decision-making process, my heart was already filled with a desire I could not ignore.

Just as there were many reasons why I shouldn't even have considered the whole idea, there were other reasons why I should. In the end, I decided that I owed it to myself to at least give this option of running my full consideration before making a final decision. I'd consult with my most trusted advisors and attempt to play out different scenarios. I'd weigh the advantages and disadvantages. I'd list the potential outcomes.

My starting point is often my family when making such major decisions. We enjoyed the life we had settled into in McLean, Virginia. We loved our new house, the children were making friends in their new schools, and my husband had a rewarding I.T. position at the Department of Housing and Urban Development. While we missed our extended family back in Los Angeles, we loved our lives in D.C.—we were truly blessed. In time, we surrounded ourselves with a new family. My friends Leslie and Rebecca were like sisters and a constant presence in our home. We had active social lives and I was at the top of my career with many challenges lying ahead. If I decided to move forward, I had a feeling it would be a wrenching process.

One thing was certain: I wouldn't make this difficult decision without my family's wholehearted support. One night after we had a long dinner conversation and I was just about to finally ask the question, Carmen (then fourteen years old) piped up with our family motto: "To whom much is given, much is expected." With those words, she had crystallized the decision for me. It was not about what I could gain from this opportunity, but about the giving of myself to this potential position. My family had been given so much. Although we had had our share of hardships, our life now felt perfect. It was time for us to give back. My husband, Alex, was behind me, but he was also hopeful that after we fully considered the option, we'd stay put.

I sympathized with where he was coming from. When we moved to Virginia, we thought we were going to live there for at least seven years and so decided to take out a competitive mortgage plan; we never thought that moving back so soon would even be a possibility. The financial loss would be tremendous with the significant prepayment penalty. Of course, there was also the emotional drain that running a statewide campaign often entails. I noticed, however, that most of our considerations, when we got down to it, revolved around finances. While money was an important factor to consider, I would never allow it to inhibit me from acting. I also had learned that if you have ever made money, you'd be able to do it again. As when making other important decisions, I asked myself if I could live with the worst-case scenario. I also knew that one more often regrets what she did not do over what she did.

In the meantime, I fulfilled my Treasury responsibilities with every ounce of my energy. This meant racking up an incredible amount of frequent flyer miles on about 150 trips in nearly two years. I knew, however, that with the appointed position of treasurer, there was little I could do to help the president get reelected. As a Senate candidate, I'd be in a much better position to help, especially on women's and Latino issues. If I chose to run, the Republican Party would be sending the unequivocal message that women within the party (especially in California) could be granted a seat at the highest table. Latinos could potentially reach another milestone and immigrants would make history once again.

At this point, the idea of running took serious hold. I was lucky to have the opportunity to meet with Ken Khachigian, the brilliant political consultant who wrote speeches for President Reagan, and whom I consider my hero. Ken exuded patience, steadiness, humor, and an incredible sense of purpose. He laid out my options, and I left our initial meeting with the firm decision to run for office. I walked back to my car with an overwhelming feeling that not only was this doable, but it had to be done. I was officially on cloud nine and dreamed of becoming the first Latina U.S. senator. It was a feeling that was as exciting as it was peaceful.

At the beginning of the campaign, we had great momen-
tum. Money was flowing in from every corner of California.
Our list of supporters grew and it wasn't just Republicans,
but many Independents and Democrats. Then, all of a sudden, something totally unanticipated happened. The recall
of the sitting governor Gray Davis took place and Arnold
Schwarzenegger—the newly elected governor—endorsed
my opponent in the primary. This was something that no
sitting governor had ever done before. The political tide was
set against our campaign.

Eric Casts His First Vote

There were photographers waiting for me to go to the polls to
cast my vote for the Republican nomination for the U.S.
Senate. I was as nervous as any candidate would be expected
to be. Even though I was down in the polls and the likelihood
of my actually becoming the nominee was slim, I nevertheless
was excited about the monumental day ahead of me. Yes,
soon the campaign would be over, but there was something
even more special taking place today. Eric, who had turned
eighteen in October, would be voting for the first time.

When we entered the polling place, Alex, Eric, and I
were greeted by smiling poll workers. It was a special
moment—not just because I was a candidate for the U.S.
Senate, but also because Eric was at my side. I was moved to
tears inside the booth. I could never have imagined eighteen
years ago when I held him in my arms that both of us would
be here.

It is during these precise moments that I realize my life has unfolded exactly as it should have. I realized that every step I had taken in my life led me to this particular moment with Eric just a few steps away voting for me. Although I was certain of the election's outcome, I also knew that everything in my life had happened exactly as it should have. There was peace in my heart.

Defeat, but Not Defeated

Although we braved the changing tides with all our efforts, I did not win the primary. While I was personally disappointed, I did not feel defeated. I had made a valiant effort in my pursuit of a historic endeavor. I worked harder than at any other time in my life—right up until eight o'clock in the evening when the election polls closed.

I didn't know at the time what my future would hold, but I was confident that I would always work in public service either as an appointed or elected official. I knew that each position prepared me for the next, whatever that should be. Living with Eric—who had faced death six times—had taught me the value of today. If I focus on doing the best I can in the present, I trust that tomorrow and the next day will fall into place. Not worrying about the future liberates my energy to focus on the now. I know many politicians spend considerable energy plotting out their every move and doing whatever it takes to ensure they get votes. I have chosen not to live my life in this manner.

I don't know where my life will take me next, but I do

know that the last time I filled out a job application was in 1979 for City National Bank. After that, all of my positions came to me. This was not a matter of plotting, but of being vigilant about opportunities that will continue my mission in life: to leave the world a better place for children like Eric and other families like ours. As with many good stories, this one comes full circle.

12. Mexican Homecoming

When I had only been the Treasurer of the United States for a few weeks—before I ran for Senate—I received a phone call from the White House to invite me to fly with President George W. Bush and President Vicente Fox aboard Air Force One. We were headed to Toledo, Ohio, for a dual presidential welcoming reception, which thousands of Latinos had been invited to attend. It made sense that, as the first Mexican-born treasurer of the U.S., I would be invited to attend. The date was set for me to meet them at Andrews Air Force base in Virginia.

I needed to share my excitement. I called my husband. I was in disbelief. How could I possibly be flying with not just one president, but two? This would be my first trip aboard Air Force One, and I wanted to soak in every second because who knew if I'd ever have such an opportunity again? Of course, I tossed and turned the entire night before the flight as I played over every minute detail in my mind, from what I would wear to what I would say. I knew a lot of people would be watching and I couldn't help but feel simultaneously self-conscious and excited. My mind wandered back to when I was just twelve years old and dreamed of soaring among the clouds as an airline stewardess. Even at that time, I felt this was just a fantasy because my parents didn't have the money to send me off to school.

As I took my seat on Air Force One, I felt a deep gratitude. It was one of those moments when how far I had come stared me in the face. I would never even have dreamed of one day flying with the president of my mother country and the president of my adoptive mother country. All around me was a whole entourage attending to every imaginable detail. There was a sophisticated communication system of telephones, faxes, and computers that allow the president to conduct business as though he were sitting in the White House. I could barely contain my excitement and couldn't wait to tour the three floors of this famous aircraft. In the meantime, I sat back and enjoyed a conversation with the two presidents.

A Grateful Daughter Returns

A second invitation—which led to one of my most cherished memories—came from President Vicente Fox in March of 2002 when I was still treasurer. President Fox requested my presence at his residence in Los Pinos to celebrate International Women's Day. Two days before the event, I was scheduled to be in Guadalajara to receive an award; I decided to contact the embassy to arrange a visit to my junior high school.

I hadn't been back to visit my school since graduating in June of 1972, and now here I was returning in a motorcade as treasurer. Although I was only fourteen years old at the time, some of my fondest memories are from my school days. As we approached the site, I turned to the driver:

"I don't want to disturb the school's schedule, but I hope they'll allow me to take pictures with some of the students," I said. "Oh, and it would be great if the principal was there so I can shake his hand."

He laughed.

"What's so funny?" I asked.

"I meant no disrespect, ma'am," he said, "but you'll see."

"What will I see exactly?"

He didn't respond, but only made my window go down from the front. The wind blew in my face and I noticed hundreds of people crowded outside my former school. An entire army of reporters armed with cameras and microphones stood around.

"There must be some sort of political rally going on," I said. I recalled how common political rallies were when I was a student there.

"Must be," he said.

We slowly made our way through the crowd, and when we arrived at the school's gates everyone began to clap and cheer; the sound was overwhelming. And then, I heard the crowd repeating my name. I felt as though my chest would cave in.

"Is this for—" I couldn't even get my words out.

"Yes, ma'am, this is all to welcome you," said the driver with a wide smile.

I was in such shock that when they opened my door, an older gentleman had to help me out of the car.

"Do you not recognize me, dear?" the man said.

I looked into his eyes and as soon as he smiled it was as though I had been transported back in time.

"Mr. Enrique Barron!" I couldn't believe it.

Mr. Barron had taught biology and was my favorite teacher. Thirty years had passed, but what I saw was the impeccably dressed teacher that all the young girls always giggled around and all the boys wanted to emulate.

He gave me a strong hug and whispered that there weren't words to describe how proud he was of me. I couldn't stop crying.

"Mi'jita, si no paras de llorar, me vas a hacer llorar a mi también," he said, warning me that if I didn't stop crying, he would have no choice but to cry as well. I doubted whether I would be able to hold myself upright if I let go.

Although I had not stayed in touch with many of my childhood friends, their faces were sprinkled throughout the crowd. I was hugging people left and right; I couldn't believe this warm reception. I came upon dignitaries and representatives from all levels of the government. Welcome banners flapped in the wind and music played. On either side of me were uniformed students in perfect lines. I made a great effort to speak with as many of them as possible. I'm sure many of the students had no idea what the big fuss was about. And yet, others had eyes that burned with the same hope mine did at their age.

The formal ceremony began in the school yard. The honor guard (a ceremonial unit dressed in uniform) marched with the Mexican flag while the national anthem was played. I remembered when I, too, proudly carried the

Mexican flag as a member of the honor guard. I saw the past and the present transpose themselves as another honor guard marched toting the U.S. flag. When the U.S. flag was passing by the Mexican flag, the Mexican flag was made to bow slightly to suggest a reverence and salutation to the U.S. flag. I gasped. There could not have been a more thoughtful way of honoring who I was. It was a moment that will forever live on in my memory until the day I die.

Every major news organization covered this momentous event. Photos were taken and headlines were written.

The story I have written is one that both begins and ends here. It's a story that has been told by many before me because it is part of the larger story of a nation that promises a dream. I had graduated from a poor school in a poor barrio in Mexico and returned thirty years later as a grateful daughter. The years in between were filled with the most vivid dream I could have hoped for, one that I hope I never wake up from.

13. Blazing a Trail

Embarking on new terrain is often as exhilarating as it is frightening. The initial rush of excitement is exactly what you'll need to get you started, but it is your ability to face challenges that lie before you that will determine your success. Oftentimes, we are our own worst enemy when our faith in our abilities is tested. How you address your own fears, how much caution you exercise, and how much risk you are willing to take—these are all questions you will face repeatedly. The sooner you can work through your own inner demons, the better off you'll be. While I would never claim to be an expert on life, I do hope that sharing my experiences and how I navigated through difficult events will better help you in your own endeavors, whether personal, professional, or both.

Everyone draws his or her strength from different sources. I know that when I've needed additional strength, I've looked to trusted friends, family, and faith in a higher power. If quitting ever crossed my mind, I thought of how much easier it would be for others if I blazed a trail, clearing the way for them to follow in my footsteps. Take comfort in knowing that once you've been the first at anything, you'll become adept at anticipating common obstacles. You'll learn how to handle dealing with stereotypes that others may project onto you. Remember that you only have control over how you live *your* life, and attempting to control others is a futile effort.

The path you walk will, inevitably, lead to some disappointments. While you'll learn how to deal with your own dashed hopes, know that, more often than not, it will be more difficult to deal with others disappointing you. Sometimes even your friends—or people you thought were your friends—will upset you. As hard as it may be, try not to dwell on these moments that you have no control over. Don't forget to keep on moving: the path you blaze for others will be its own reward. Everything in life comes at a price, and that includes the privileged role of being the first.

In my life, it started with being the first and only member of my family to graduate from college. Without accomplishing this important task, it is highly doubtful that many other professional "firsts" would have followed. My next first was as a mother of a child with disabilities to serve as chief of legislative affairs for the Department of Developmental Services. This opportunity was a blend of the personal and professional because it arose from discovering that my mission in life is to leave the world a better place for families like mine that have children with disabilities. The list of firsts continued: the first woman in our city council, first Latina chair of the State Council on Developmental Disabilities, first immigrant to become treasurer of the United States, and, finally, the first Latina in California to run for a U.S. Senate position.

Every time I've been the first to try anything, I am cognizant of both the privilege and the responsibility that it entails. As I pursue any position, I'm fully aware of its import. There have been many people who have been by my side and have wanted me to succeed. But there were just as many people who would have been delighted to see me fail. I knew that my success would breed success for others that followed. On the other hand, if I had failed, it would have meant closing the door for someone after me—especially other Latinas. This knowledge, coupled with the weight of this responsibility, has provided the adrenaline I have needed to stay focused and succeed time and time again. I've already shared my life with you, but let's zoom in on the specific moments when I was faced with the challenge of being first. It is my hope that I will inspire you to embark on whatever challenge lies before you today and in the future—regardless of whether it has been attempted before. Either way, it will be the first time you have tried it.

The First to Graduate from College

Let's start with my education. Being the first in my family to graduate from college required that I place familial and personal expectations in perspective. Both of my parents had a six-year education and to see almost all their children graduate from high school surpassed what they thought was possible. I was fortunate to be able to rely on my family for emotional support. I remember my *tia* Josefina in Mexico who used to shower me with praise, telling everyone and anyone how proud she was of my scholastic achievements, like being in the honor guard. In the United States, my family knew how important an education could be in an abstract sort of way, but I didn't have the benefit of the concrete support mechanisms that are in place within other families that have achieved higher levels of education for generations.

It was a turning point for me when I had a teacher in the U.S. laugh along with the class at how low my IQ test results were. Of course, it can prove difficult to take a test when one doesn't understand the language it is written in. Although that is still a painful memory, it has also been the gift that keeps on giving. I had something to prove and although it began with an external event, it quickly became a matter of proving it to myself. I was driven and never satisfied, despite surpassing all expectations. In the end, we have to be honest with ourselves about how few people truly care about whether we attain a higher level of education. Education is its own reward, with the by-product being the success that follows when it is put to good use in the world. I know that my parents (at the time) questioned why I felt it was so important to graduate from college. It was only after they saw how far I was able to run with my education that they understood. They were proud that they raised a tenacious daughter who could take responsibility for her own success. You must do the same, even if those around you don't expect anything better from you. Although it is always nice to hear praise and to receive accolades, the best reward is your own self-improvement.

Once I attained my degree, I was not satisfied. I looked behind me and saw that my siblings would soon be standing where I was. When my youngest sister Nancy graduated from high school, I gave her a car so that she could commute to college. I let her know that she could benefit from my experience and that if she should need anything, I would be a pillar of support. The car was simply a tool that would enable her to commute. She had everything she needed to succeed, and yet, she decided not to finish her degree at the time. Of course, I was disappointed. I didn't have any role models and I had to work hard to purchase my first car. I realized then that I did everything I could for my sister and, ultimately, we all have to live with our decisions. A few years ago, Nancy decided to go back and try to finish her degree. For her own sake, I hope she does.

Today, each time I greet any one of my twenty-one nephews and nieces with a "good morning" or "good afternoon," a barrage follows: "How's school? How are you doing in math and English? Which college are you going to attend?" No matter what their answers are, I make sure to stress the importance of an education. If they are behind, let's get them some tutors. If they are bored, maybe they aren't being challenged. It is no longer an option not to have a college education, and there is certainly no excuse for not pursuing one. Having been the first, I make it clear that I will do everything in my power to ensure their success.

With the challenge of being the first at anything also comes a set of exhilarating opportunities. Any success that follows not only benefits you, but also serves as an example to those who anticipate similar barriers. That you never give in to your fears or give up will not only serve you, but will also inspire others to the same success. There is nothing more touching than when I meet other Latinas who have the same drive to succeed as I do. I'm flattered when they say that they want to be just like me. No matter how busy I am, I'll take the time to offer encouraging words. I try to convey that although it has rarely been easy for me, the fact that I was able to succeed means they can too. There is a famous saying in the Latino community: *¡Si se puede!* (Yes it can be done!) It's a rallying cry popularized by activist Cesar Chavez. I often tell young Latino students that they can achieve whatever their hearts desire. Of course, Latino parents need to be able to let go. It especially pains me to hear about young Latinas who are offered college scholarships but do not accept them because their parents want them to stay close to home. In Mexico, a young girl will often not leave home until her wedding day. This is the U.S., however, and without the degree, opportunities are limited. Again, we are sometimes our own worst enemies.

I hope that the life I have led serves as an example and adds credibility to my advice. I tell other Latinos that I came from a poor family and was never offered any scholarships or grants. It may have taken me a long time to complete my education, but the bottom line is that I stuck with it and graduated. If it is possible for me, then certainly it is possible for them. Oftentimes it is knowing that you will not be the first that provides the comfort and confidence that is needed to get started.

First Latina and Mother of a Child with Disabilities to Become Chief of Legislative Affairs for the DDS

I'm a proud Latina who has worked hard to get to where she is. And yet, some people told me that the only reason I've been offered positions is specifically because of my ethnicity. I have dealt with the "she got there because she's Latina" syndrome more times than I care to count. When I became the first mother of a child with disabilities to be appointed chief of legislative affairs for the Department of Developmental Services, a colleague of mine told me: "They only brought you here because you're Latina." What made her comment particularly painful was that she was also a Latina. It took me a while before I realized she was only projecting her level of self-hate onto me. She didn't bother to check my experience. It didn't matter to her that I had created an entire Spanish-language support network for Latino families of children with Down syndrome. Never mind that I led an effort to successfully lobby the legislature for improved services for our children. It didn't matter that I spent years as a volunteer advocate for my community. It may have been too difficult for her to understand that I had more to offer in my position as a mother and advocate than I could ever offer from solely being a Latina.

Initially, these types of comments were painful to stomach. After that first encounter, two other Latinas in Sacramento joined the chorus by suggesting that the governor was using my Latina status for his own purposes. I went home and cried. They tried to tear me down psychologically, and in the beginning, they succeeded. But then I realized that the nature of politics had more to do with those comments than reality did. The only difference was that they were Democrats and I was a Republican. We were all Latinas in positions of influence, but they chose to be consumed by envy and jealousy. I chose not to retaliate by turning their questions back on them. I made a firm decision not to stoop down to their level. There will be many times when people will poke and prod you with the hopes that you'll join them in a fight. It's best to learn which fights are worth your time and effort.

I needed to process that initial discriminatory experience to be ready for the next that followed shortly after. This time when it was intimated that I got to where I was because I was Latina, I simply smiled and said, "I sure hope so." Those four words immediately disarmed the offender, who expected to offend. Today, I know enough about politics and, more importantly, about myself that if anybody suggests that I got anywhere because I'm Latina, I just laugh them off.

First Woman and Latina to Serve on the Huntington Park City Council

There were two women, both Latinas, elected to the city council for the first time in 1994. Because I received more votes than the other woman and was immediately named mayor pro tem, I bore the brunt of the degrading comments from a longtime council member. Most of the time, I was able to ignore his remarks about women and minorities because it was clear to me that he was a relic with eyes closed to the realities of our city. He was seldom successful in getting under my skin because, instead of anger, he evoked pity. It was fitting, then, that the end of his career was precipitated by derogatory comments he made about Latinos. It was a valuable lesson: sometimes if we let enough time pass, we will see people who have hurt us bring about their own demise. If we give them enough rope, they'll eventually hang themselves.

First Latina Chair of the State Council on Developmental Disabilities

When I was elected chair of the council, the political forces against Governor Wilson suggested that he was only using me because I was Latina. Again, I realized that it had nothing to do with me, but with the fact that the governor was a Republican placing another Republican in a position of influence.

I learned to deal with the comments in a matter-of-fact way. It would be a waste of my time to try to convince anyone about my qualifications. That energy would be better utilized in accomplishing my goals. Once I let go of any need to justify my appointment, I felt liberated. I also learned that there are people who have low self-esteem and feel the need to put others down to feel superior. The only proper reaction, I found, was to feel sorry for them.

First Immigrant to Become Treasurer of the United States

As the first immigrant to become treasurer of the United States, I made history. For me, it was the culmination of a career in public service. What should have been a purely celebratory event for immigrants around the country—especially Latinos—was tainted a bit when the Latina remarks began to prey on me again like parasites.

Shortly after my appointment, a highly regarded reporter in Mexico asked me what I thought of the critics who suggested I was offered the position only because I was a Latina. What did I do? Of course, I flashed a wide smile and said: "I should hope so!" He laughed and the interview moved on. I've reached a point in my life where ignorance doesn't offend me because I'm able to find the humor in it. Laughter when appropriately aimed can be the greatest weapon in your arsenal.

What I've learned—at times painfully—is that there will always be some aspect of who you are that can be seized upon by others in an attempt to break your spirit. Some of these attempts will be subtle and some will be overt. Whatever you do, don't give anyone the power to make you question your race, gender, party affiliation, social status, or anything else for that matter. There are naysayers who will grab at your ankles on your way up, but it's up to you to kick them aside.

First Latina in California to Run for U.S. Senate

When I was running for the U.S. Senate, a Latino Democratic member suggested that I was the house-Mexican of the Republican Party. Once again, it was one of my own who would've liked to see me fail. He, admittedly, saw himself as the manservant of the Democratic Party and felt that he could impose his own low self-worth onto me. Incidentally, this was just a few months after Harry Belafonte compared Colin Powell to a house slave. Although that was also an unjustified statement, it made me feel as though I was in good company.

Of course, as a Latina, a lot of people expected me to be a registered Democrat. Somewhere people have developed the mistaken belief that because I'm both an immigrant and a Latina, I have no choice in my party affiliation. Unfortunately, it often seems that unless you're a Democrat, you're going to be seen as less of a Latino. I don't know when it became acceptable for people to question your ethnicity based on your party affiliation, but it's something I have faced often.

Everything that is worthwhile has a price and that includes political participation. Finger-pointing and snide remarks are a small price to pay to ensure that as a community, Latinos are represented in the two major political parties. I have often joked that I get invited to speak at many Latino nonprofit events because I fulfill their nonpartisan quota. In all seriousness, however, I believe that people should be judged based on their actions. Anyone looking at my history will see that each time I have attained positions of influence, I've been able to deliver services and programs for the Latino community. This should ultimately be more important than whether I am a Republican or a Democrat.

It is my own actions that have ensured I've earned my achievements. No one has ever handed me anything on a silver platter and it was years before I could afford to buy one of my own. I make no excuses for my successes because I've attained them the old-fashioned way: through hard work. I'd understand these criticisms if I hadn't fought tooth and nail to get to where I was. I've always prided myself in having worked harder than anyone I knew in all of the positions I've held. I made sure that I was always the first one in and the last one out of the office.

I've had to develop a thick skin and so must you. I've told people throughout the years that my mom must've given me many oil baths when I was a child because nothing sticks to me. There have been countless times when I've been singled out and have had to navigate the murky waters of self-doubt. With time, it has become easier to successfully deal with my minority status—as an immigrant in school, as a young immigrant Latina working in a Beverly Hills bank, as a Republican in a Democratic city . . . the list goes on.

What I desire more than anything else is to ensure I leave all of the doors of opportunity open behind me. In order to do this, I've had some wise mentors hold doors open for me, but only after I've initially opened them. I suggest you also seek out people who are doing what you'd like to do or are living the type of life you imagine for yourself. Once you find these mentors, cling to them until you've learned everything you possibly can. By the same token, make sure to train anyone who you hope will replace you as you continue on your path. It has always been of the utmost importance for me to train my replacements. I learned long ago that it wasn't acceptable for me to hear, "How can we promote you when there's no one to do your job?" I figured out that the best answer to this question was to prepare someone else for my position. This ensured that the next time an opportunity arose, I'd be considered for a higher position.

I'm fond of saying that we can no longer concern ourselves with just overcoming barriers, but instead, we need to eliminate them for the next generation that will follow. This ensures that its energy will be spent on achieving even greater things than we have been able to. So I'm going to ask you to help the next person achieve his or her goals. If someone has helped you reach where you are today, consider giving back.

If you are still on your way to achieving the American Dream, read on for the successful seven actions that will help you on your journey.

14. The Successful Seven

I n this final section, I'd like to share the seven most important actions that I have repeatedly carried out to achieve success. Like anything else, the more often you take these actions, the more adept you will become at their application. No one necessarily starts a journey equipped with everything he or she needs, but it is my hope that these successful seven will act as your guideposts. These actions are suggestive of certain values that have guided, sustained, and carried me throughout the years. Although many people claim to hold a certain value dear, it isn't until they have been tested that they can confidently say they truly possess it. It has been during the most difficult moments of my life—when I have been tested by circumstances beyond my control—that these actions have come to my rescue.

I've found that the best advice is direct, simple, and immediately applicable to any facet of your life. I don't believe that you can be one kind of person in public and another in private: I am only one individual regardless of my setting. I've read plenty of books in which advice is dispensed without examples. Since you're already familiar with several of the pivotal moments in my life, I'll backtrack a bit to further explore the other dimensions of these events. It is my hope that my experiences will help you if you are ever confronted with similar challenges.

Without further ado:

1. Always do the right thing.
2. Always try your best.
3. Always treat people the way you'd like to be treated.
4. Listen to yourself.
5. Choose carefully, then act.
6. As hard as it may be, fake courage.
7. When you attain power, be sure to use it.

1. Always Do the Right Thing.

As you approach the small and large tasks that make up ordinary and extraordinary efforts, there will be times when you'll be tempted to do something that you know is not right. I always remember the advice that the assembly-woman gave me when we faced the budget crisis: Draw a line and do not cross it. You, too, must draw your own lines.

The temptation to act against your own internal voice will be especially strong when no one is looking. I grew up with the fundamental understanding that it is at these times that your values are truly tested. In politics, there have been many potential exits that could have, perhaps, been beneficial on other levels. I know, however, that I must face myself at the end of the day. Regardless of whether anyone will notice, you'll ultimately have to live with your decisions. If you can look at yourself in the mirror with pride, then you can take even the most devastating loss with dignity.

In almost every speech I give, I highlight the fact that people can take away your house, your position, everything you own, but no one can take away your integrity. Only you can chisel it away. This can happen in the subtlest ways on both conscious and subconscious levels. You must not only resist, but also guard your integrity with all of your might. Even the most solid integrity will crumble if your own actions chisel away at it. There have been countless times in my life when it would have been easier to simply go with the flow and not do what I knew was right. It was during these moments that my character was tested. I'll share just a few of these moments with you.

An Assemblywoman's Advice

"I always draw a line and promise myself that no matter what, I will not cross it. That also means that I never move the line to accommodate my current situation because that's the same thing as crossing the line. I'm also careful not to come up with excuses for moving the line. Once you do that, then you have to ask yourself, when will I stop?"

These helpful words stayed with me long after I left the assemblywoman's office. I went to her for advice when the proposal that was to be submitted would have severely weakened the system for those with disabilities. Her words gave me the courage to make the decision that crystallized who I was. What drove me each day was my need to do what was right. In this particular context, that meant staying true to my mission of helping people like my son Eric and their families.

It is often the case that in the heat of legislative wars, if people are not willing to take a stand, the most vulnerable suffer. I'm content that this wasn't the case this time around.

Proposition 187

I could no longer hide how I truly felt about the proposition that would deny services to thousands of undocumented immigrants. Although I knew it went against the Republican political tide, I could not live with myself if I let myself get carried away by it. I mustered enough courage to stand in front of all my colleagues and say: "I want all of you to know that I'll do everything in my power to get the governor reelected, but I'm also taking a stand against Proposition 187. I will fight just as adamantly to defeat it."

I also implored them to remove from the airwaves the black-and-white commercial of Latino children in the classroom. The commercial implied that tax dollars shouldn't fund the education of undocumented children. I know my voice cracked and my knees wobbled, but what's important is that I said what needed to be said. There was absolute silence in the room as I took my seat. The person briefing us on the governor's campaign reminded me that the ad buys were separate from the 187 campaign. The governor had nothing to do with the commercials. He did, however, understand the situation and asked if there were other people who felt the same way. Although hesitant at first, others began to chime in. Looking around the room, I was very proud of my Latino counterparts. It was clear that this was painful for all of us. Children should be off the table, we explained. He promised us he'd check into it and relay the messages that we had delivered. He'd do anything he could to stop that commercial. A couple of days later, it was off the air.

It would have been easier for me to say nothing about how I truly felt about Proposition 187 and the offensive commercial. I was beginning to get the feeling that taking the right action often led to discomfort. In this case, I had to speak up for the voiceless who were not in that room—even if that meant losing the esteem of my Republican colleagues. I ran the risk of being alienated and labeled a traitor. But, I had to be honest with them and (more importantly) with myself.

I have found time and time again that when you stand up for what you believe in, people will respect you and some may even change their minds and agree with you. What's important is not only which action you choose to take, but also how you explain your point of view to those around you. I try to make my arguments by painting a picture that overflows with my passions and convictions. Remember that people most likely will be left with not only what you said, but also how it was said. My feelings always come to the surface. It is rare for anyone to have a doubt in his or her mind as to where I stand on an issue.

Soul: Not for Sale

I had a chance to take the easy way out that day when an influential Democratic Party member met with me. After explaining how Governor Wilson was not the right candidate for the Latino community, she asked that I renounce my party affiliation and support the governor's opponent. In exchange, she guaranteed that I'd be made an assemblywoman at the earliest possible election. Of course, at the time, I was offended. But then, I realized my husband was right: many people in that same situation would have given up what they believed in to secure a higher office.

Like I've said, everything has a price. There will always be people willing to sell their souls if the price is right. These people will sell their convictions for a myriad of reasons. I made the decision long ago that no price is high enough and I suggest you do the same. Sticking by your beliefs and convictions will have a more handsome payout in the end. I know that I wouldn't be able to live with myself had I turned on the governor. I know that a decision like that would have led to inner turmoil. As far as I'm concerned, no office is worth the price of sleepless nights. The governor only found out about this incident long after he left office. My decision was not based on what would further my own career, but on what I felt was the right course of action.

Inviting Governor Wilson to Huntington Park

Taking the right action in this particular case involved doing everything I could to stop the Huntington Park's crime problem. Most of the incidents were a result of gang violence. Each day brought more senseless drive-by shootings, the deaths of precious children, and murders. I didn't need to read the paper or tune into the news—the effects were all around me. Lowering the crime rate was far more important to me than getting reelected to the city council. I knew that many political leaders and citizens would be against my bringing Governor Wilson to Huntington Park. There was still a lot of palpable resentment over Proposition 187 and its effects on our community (it would later be ruled unconstitutional). Although I sympathized with where people were coming from, I also knew that the ends would justify the means. If it took bringing an unpopular politician into my city to highlight a growing problem, then so be it. I faced lots of anger and resentment in taking the right course of action.

Bringing the governor to our city did cause the crime rate to go down. Through a state program, the federal government gave our city three helicopters that were used for air patrolling. There was a significant drop in gang violence. I did my job by doing what I thought was in the best interest of my city. Taking the right action paid off: the crime rate dropped and the citizens expressed their gratitude by reelecting me.

2. Always Try Your Best.

No matter how small the job or how menial the chore, you must always try your best. This is especially true in cases when you could get away with doing less. Your best may vary from one day to the next, but as long as you are trying, there is nothing more that can be asked of you. Even if you fall short of somebody's expectations, you should never fall short of your own. Even if you do not "succeed" according to someone else, at least you have not failed yourself. Ultimately, a job well done is its own best reward.

The Rose Fitzgerald Kennedy Prize

One day Denny Amundson—the director of the Department

of Developmental Services—called me into his office to tell me that he had nominated me to receive the Rose Fitzgerald Kennedy Prize. At the time I had never heard of this prize, but I was flattered that he thought so highly of my work to nominate me. Once I learned about the Joseph P. Kennedy, Jr. Foundation and its international awards, the mere thought of a nomination was an honor. At this point, I had a lot on my plate. I had worked for the DDS for almost two years and we had been successful in reforming the entire system in California. I chaired the State Council on Developmental Disabilities and had been elected to the city council. Throughout it all, I remained involved in FUERZA, the volunteer organization that I had created to support Spanish-speaking families of children with disabilities.

Even considering all these accomplishments, how could I ever receive an award named for a woman who had made such an impact on the lives of children with disabilities all around the world? There was simply no way I could compare with the achievements of such a magnificent human being. I thought this must be how actors feel when they are nominated for an Oscar.

A few months went by before I received a call from the foundation. I waited for a few seconds for Eunice Kennedy Shriver's secretary to transfer me to her line. In a calm voice she said that her siblings had reviewed all the applications the previous night and all agreed that I should receive the award that honored her mother. She went on to explain that this year's award was especially significant because her mother had passed away at the beginning of the year.

"I wanted to talk with you personally," she said. "I was

touched by all of the things you've done as a result of your son's having Down syndrome."

"I was just doing what I felt needed to be done," I said.

"And that is exactly what reminded me of my own mother," she said. "My sister Rosemary was a source of inspiration for her and the reason she decided to advocate and create programs for people with mental retardation.

I was honored that she would even compare me with her own mother. She began to read the nomination papers that Denny had submitted. She listed my various accomplishments and said that she was pleased to learn about the combination of public policy and politics in my background. She talked about how her mother influenced President Kennedy to protect people with disabilities and why we need people in politics who understand those needs. She was touched that I had chosen to help people who only spoke Spanish. She understood how much more difficult it must be for people who do not speak English to access the necessary services for their children. She was also impressed by the special masses we held for families. She shared that her mother was Catholic and that the foundation had created a catechism for the mentally retarded. She also mentioned how her mother was the real political person in the family. She liked the fact that I had been elected to the city council and often spoke about the power of government to do good.

I was speechless. What an incredible distinction to be recognized for my work, especially in such an unexpected way. I told her how undeserving I felt, especially when compared to her mother's accomplishments. I reiterated that I only had done what I saw needed to be done. My accomplishments were the result of fulfilling welcomed obligations. When my son was born and there were no Spanish-speaking support groups, I knew what I had to do. It had always been this way: come across an unfulfilled need and get down to work.

As I finished the conversation with Mrs. Shriver, she told me to hold on the line for the executive director who would make the travel arrangements for me to fly to New York with my family. The ceremony would take place in July of 1995, on the eve of the International Symposium on the Rights of People with Mental Retardation at the United Nations. I would be there with representatives from around the world and other international award recipients. I was told that my award would be the last of the evening. The director asked for the name of a family who could provide testimony of how I had helped them through the FUERZA support group. My mind began to reel. The group had helped so many families throughout the years that it was difficult to narrow it down. He prodded me to find one where it had made a significant difference.

We decided to ask the Alcaraz family if they'd like to come with us to New York. They also lived in Huntington Park and our families had grown close throughout the years. When we arrived at the ceremony in New York, Ana wasn't able to say what she needed to because her English wasn't strong enough. Her husband, Ignacio, spoke for the family. They shared how she contacted me when her baby girl Gaby was born with Down syndrome and she couldn't stand the thought of taking care of her. She had asked her mother to come from Mexico with the intention of having baby Gaby go back with her. She shared how her mother would stay in the bedroom all day with the baby. No matter how hard Ana tried, she could not bring herself to hold Gaby in her arms. She didn't want anything to do with her baby. Arrangements had already been made for her mother to take the baby back to Mexico. As the day approached, the guilt began to crush her.

When I first visited Ana in her home, I asked to see the baby. When the grandmother came out of the bedroom cradling Gaby, I asked if I could hold her. I took Gaby carefully and looked into her beautiful eyes and started in with cooing and baby talk. Gaby laughed uncontrollably. Ana's astonishment was immeasurable. She looked puzzled, as if asking me: "How could you talk to *that* baby like it were any other baby?" Ana didn't yet understand how Gaby deserved the same kind of attention that any other baby did. Gaby was a baby, first and foremost. Yes, she did have Down syndrome, but that was secondary. I held Gaby in my arms for a long time while talking to Ana. She knew that I understood everything she was going through. I had gone through many of the similar feelings of rejection when Eric was born. My friend Elise had been there for me to let me know it was okay, and now I hoped to do the same for Ana.

When I went to give Gaby back to Ana instead of the grandmother, Ana's initial reaction was hesitation. I asked her to please hold the baby. She seemed shy at first, almost afraid. When she finally extended her arms to take Gaby, tears began to flow, and they did not stop for a long time. She was overwhelmed with guilt—I told her I understood. After that day, she said that she wouldn't even think of giving up Gaby. For the first time ever, Gaby slept in Ana's bedroom that night.

That one visit had changed this family's life. Had I not

gone to visit them, Gaby most likely would've gone to live with her grandmother in Mexico. She would never have had the chance to develop relationships with her mother, father, and siblings. She would have faded into the recesses of the family's memory, never to be spoken about, like she was a shameful secret.

Everything That Leaves My Desk Has My Signature

Seated at my desk, I waited for the vice president of the bank, Mr. Kyman, to sign the letter I had typed for him earlier in the day. Toward the end of my shift, he called me into his office and asked that I sit down. That is rarely a good sign. I braced myself for a verbal whipping. He told me that he was disappointed to find a typo in the letter he had dictated to me. He handed the sheet back to me and said that he'd never sign anything that had any errors in it because it reflected poorly on him. More importantly, he said, I should never give him anything that has a typo in it because it also reflected poorly on me. He went on to say the words that have been engraved in my memory ever since: "Everything that leaves my desk has my signature on it and as such reflects the kind of work I do. Therefore, it must be excellent."

He said that he never expected perfection, but he did expect excellence. If he couldn't trust me with a small task like checking the spelling of a letter, then how could he trust me with something bigger? He went on to explain how each one of us has talents and we should be given the opportunities to use them. He could see that I had potential, but slipshod work would discredit my efforts. He had expected better from me and was, consequently, upset.

I left his office shaking. Instead of being angry, I quietly condemned myself for not being more thorough. Something like a typo seemed like the smallest mistake, but what it represented was not. I knew he was right, and I was genuinely appreciative of the lesson. If he couldn't trust me with small things, then how could I expect him to trust me with more important tasks? I was upset, but I promised myself that from that point on, I'd check and recheck anything leaving my desk. Even if the work didn't always carry my physical signature, it did carry my stamp of excellence.

As I moved up in my professional life, I made sure to share that anecdote with my coworkers and employees. Ever since that day, I take on every task—no matter how small— with great dedication, enthusiasm, and commitment.

The Goal Is Excellence, Not Perfection

Since I always try my best, I expect others who are part of my team to do so as well. I also believe that people will more often than not meet your expectations if they are clearly explained. Oftentimes, people actually surprise me and perform far better than I anticipate. Consequently I expect the best from everyone I come in contact with. I usually give them "the talk" about my expectations during our first meeting; it always ends with: "I expect excellence, not perfection."

I make a very clear distinction between the two. When one expects excellence in performance, imperfect outcomes are allowed. But if one expects perfection, then things like unforeseen circumstances that are beyond our control are not allowed. When one expects excellence, it often leads to fulfillment. On the other hand, when one expects perfection, it more often than not will lead to frustration and resentment.

I was amazed when I first learned that Thomas Edison failed fifty-eight hundred times before he perfected the light bulb. When asked how he felt about those thousands of failed attempts, he answered that it wasn't failure at all because he learned that there are thousands of ways that light cannot be produced. Rather than seeing his attempts as failures, he chose to view them as learning experiences.

Going to Harvard

Some of the most meaningful moments in my life occurred because I've willed them into existence through persistence and perseverance. In most cases, if you keep at it and never give up, it has to happen. I had always wondered what it would be like to go to Harvard University. There were times when both my husband and I would dream out loud (during late-night study sessions) about what it would be like to attend the first established U.S. university. Of course these were pipe dreams as there was simply no way it would be possible. We were already married, and we both led busy lives. Our time had come and gone.

But one day, my boss Denny went to a three-week summer program for senior executives at the John F. Kennedy School of Government at Harvard University. When he returned, he regaled us with tales of how wonderful his experience had been. He told his executive committee how rewarding it was and that if we should ever be able to go, we certainly should. A light flicked on in my head. If Denny had gone, maybe I could go, too. I immediately asked him what it would take for me to be admitted into the program.

He politely told me that there were other people on the executive team who were already scheduled to go, that it was expensive, and that it was competitive to get into. Although he didn't kill all my hopes, he did say that there was no way it would happen in the foreseeable future.

The following year, I asked again and was denied. The year after that, I was at the state council and, because it was not a full-time job, the state couldn't pay my way. No matter which position I found myself in, I continued to ask if I could attend the Harvard program. When I was at the Department of Social Services, I asked the director of the department. She said that she would give me the time off, but I'd have to pay the tuition. I knew the program was expensive (around eight thousand dollars) but decided that I had persevered and no time was better than the present. Unfortunately, I was moved into the governor's office before I had a chance to attend. When I told my new boss that I already had plans to attend, she initially agreed, but then she decided that we were simply too busy for me to take time off. I was very disappointed because she was going back on our agreement. She promised me that I'd certainly go next year.

At that point, it was the governor's last year in office and I knew it would be my last opportunity to attend the three-week program. Since my boss had promised me the prior year, I knocked on her door to remind her that I was going to apply. Although she was hesitant at first, I reminded her of our agreement. Besides, I told her, this would be the last year I could go because once the governor was out of office, who knew where I'd end up. She finally relented and I submitted my application.

The wait to hear back was excruciating. I knew that the program was competitive and received hundreds of applications; they make sure that anyone attending has something to contribute to the program. It was a selective process, so I tried not to get my hopes up. I was nervous the day I arrived home and saw an envelope with the Harvard insignia. I carefully opened it and unfolded an acceptance letter. I took a deep breath: I was finally going to Harvard.

When I arrived at the campus, I had to pause to acknowledge how long it had taken me to get there. I learned a lot from the teachers and students during the three weeks—lessons that have stayed with me since. The most important lesson I learned: never give up!

It would have been easy to stop trying year in and year out, but I had my sight locked onto Harvard and I knew I was worth it. Today, I proudly display my certificate of completion in a custom frame—it looks like a diploma. Although I'll never forget it's from Harvard, what it more importantly reminds me of is the power of perseverance. I could've given up on the fifth try, but the sixth attempt was a charm.

Ethnic Advisory Minority Committee

Advocating on behalf of the Latino community within the service delivery system of California was an energy-draining process. The State Council on Developmental Disabilities was the agency in charge of developing the plan to satisfy the needs of people with disabilities. I was a member of a coalition of Latino professionals who believed that Latino parents and their children were not receiving the same quality or amount of support services that other, non-Latino parents had access to. Although it was clear as day to Latinos that this was the case, there was no documentation to support our claims. There was also no documentation to prove the opposite. So we demanded that a committee be formed within the state council to analyze whether in fact what we believed was correct.

The council would have nothing to do with that request. Rather than accept defeat, we decided to raise the issue at every single council meeting. Our rationale was that they'd eventually have to honor our request to form an ethnic advisory committee. We followed the council throughout the entire state. Whenever they met, we'd address them with the exact same request. It got to the point where council members wouldn't even acknowledge our presence. During the public input period, the chair of the council would rudely tell us that the council was not going to take any action. The last time I addressed the council—against the wishes of the chair—I flatly told its members that they could mark my words: "I promise you that one way or another, there will be an ethnic minority advisory committee formed in the state of California. This is the last time I will address you, but a committee will be formed and charged with the mission you have denied us."

As luck would have it, I went to work for the Department of Developmental Services and, two years later, the governor appointed me to the State Council on Developmental Disabilities, and I was elected chair of the council. My first order of business was the creation of the ethnic minority advisory committee.

The findings of the committee verified what we had suspected all along: Latino families with children who have disabilities were not receiving the same level or amount of services that other, non-Latino families were receiving. This acknowledgment was an essential first step. Now, we were ready to build programs that were more culturally relevant to minority parents. Again, this only came to pass because I would not take no for an answer. You, too, should never accept no as an answer. Luckily, if you always try your best, you won't have to.

3. Always Treat People the Way You'd Like to Be Treated.

You must afford the same respect to the person who shines the chairwoman's shoes as you would the chairwoman of the board. Remember they are individuals, just like you. I'm sure you've heard of the Golden Rule, the Ten Commandments, and simple social manners. I'd like to think that anyone reading this book treats people with the utmost respect. When I look around, however, I can't help but feel that if people followed this one simple rule, the world would be a more peaceful place. I know how powerful this philosophy really is because I had the opportunity to observe my grandmother Juanita when I was a child. I've often said that everything I learned about politics, my grandma Juanita taught me.

My grandma only had two years of formal schooling, but she'd always remind us that "we might be poor but we must act well-educated." In Mexico, good manners equal a good education. A person could earn the recognition of being well educated if she acted politely. Well, I can tell you that my grandma had a Ph.D. in manners. Every time I accompanied her, I noticed how cordial and polite she was. The moment someone crossed our path, whether she knew them or not, my grandma would always say hello and good morning, afternoon, or evening. For the most part, everyone responded and she'd flash her smile. If we had some more time and she knew the person, she'd inquire about the person's family or simply exchange a few pleasantries. It only took a few minutes from her day, but I'm sure it made other people's days a lot more pleasant. In the unlikely event that someone chose not to acknowledge her, she'd shrug it off with a comment such as, "He must be very preoccupied with something. I hope it turns out okay for him."

She effectively impressed upon all her grandchildren—by the power of her living example—to treat everyone with respect. Respecting others and respecting myself are probably the most cherished values I grew up with—and in many ways they are one and the same. My grandma was fond of reminding us of the immortal phrase that Benito Juarez (widely considered by Mexicans to be the first president) is remembered for: *"El respeto al derecho ajeno es la paz."* That is: "Respect for others' rights is peace." I often joke with my own children that after reciting the Lord's Prayer, we had to recite this presidential quote.

Everyone Deserves to Be Acknowledged

Later on in life, I would find many instances where small, yet powerful messages would be rewarded. I often recall how when the chairman of the board of the bank would arrive in the morning and proceed to his office, everyone would greet him with a "Good morning sir, how are you?" His personal assistant—an older gentleman who had been with the chairman for a long time—would follow right behind him. I was appalled by how respect was showered upon the chairman, but few (if any) acknowledged his assistant. I always made it a point to acknowledge both of them.

One morning, when the chairman arrived without his assistant, the usual flurry of greetings began. The chairman leaned over my desk and whispered: "I just want to thank you for acknowledging my assistant. You're the only one and I really appreciate it. It means a lot to me." I was surprised that the chairman would take the time out of his schedule to thank me for something I thought of as common courtesy. In my opinion, everyone deserves at least a good morning greeting. And yet, it was clear that not everyone subscribed to this philosophy. The chairman saw his assistant—the person who would make sure his shoes were shined and that his newspaper and coffee were ready—as a valuable person. I did as well. I have often heard that one should treat the secretaries and administrative staff at companies with the greatest care because they are the gatekeepers to the rest of the company. I couldn't agree more, but I disagree with actions that have underlying motivations like having access to someone. You should treat people the way you'd like to be treated because, ultimately, it's really a reflection of how much you respect yourself.

The Campaign Trail

The lessons my grandma taught me would help me throughout my life, but they were especially useful when I was campaigning for city council. There were some days that began with breakfast with a business owner, continued with a stroll through a poor neighborhood, and then ended with *carne asada* at someone's home for dinner. I felt at home whether I was at a fancy restaurant or in someone's garage.

Some of the stories that have been written about me highlighted the fact that I walked through the poor neighborhoods of my city as though that was something extraordinary. As far as I was concerned, these were the people that I wanted to represent. They deserved to be visited by me just like any other voter. My heart would break when poor people would tell me that no one had ever visited their homes to ask for their votes. The most important thing that my grandma taught me is that people are people regardless of how much they own or how powerful they are (or seem to be). Everyone experiences fears, dreams, desires, and hopes. I feel blessed for having come from humble beginnings because I understand what it means to lack resources and can appreciate when there is an abundance of them.

I often go out of my way to acknowledge people regardless of the positions they hold. Since I work late, I usually see the janitors in my building cleaning up after everyone is long gone. No matter how busy I am, I smile and engage them in conversation. At the very least, I say hello. I treat them exactly the way I wanted people to treat my dad when he was a janitor. It was his hard work that fed our family from the time we were in Mexico and well into our lives in the U.S. He did his job with pride. He'd even give us lessons, teaching us efficient techniques to clean tiles, rugs, and mirrors. He'd tell us about how proud he felt when he left the big boss's office sparkling clean.

Till this day, if I come upon a shiny just-cleaned floor, I'll try to see if there is a detour I could take instead of walking on it. Sometimes, I wait until the floor dries. I remember that my dad would have to mop floors over and over when people walked on them. Out of sheer respect for their work, I make sure to do everything in my power to make sure janitors' lives do not need to be any more difficult. I know that I wouldn't appreciate it if someone came into my office and scattered my files. Regardless of the context, whether I'm in an office, airport, or supermarket, I treat people the way I like to be treated.

Thanking the Janitor

I'll forever be indebted to this country. It is one of the few that explicitly holds up the pursuit of happiness as an ideal. It's powerful to think that this country was founded on the idea that everyone deserves the same opportunity to reach his or her given potential. In the U.S., the concept that everyone is created equal is a part of our constitution—a documented reminder that we must treat each other with respect. I know that there have been (and still are) many cases today where ideals are not honored. There is an assurance, however, in knowing that these ideals have existed since our nation's inception and have become part of our collective culture.

I find it hard to imagine any other country where my vivid memories would have been created. I can't think of a better example than when I was being sworn in as treasurer—when I looked to the front row and saw my dad (a janitor) and my mom (a seamstress) beaming with pride as they witnessed their little girl becoming the next treasurer. Although where you come from still influences where you are going in this country, it is not impossible to rise above with some hard work. I speak English with an accent and come from humble beginnings, but that didn't stop me. Although there have been times when I've been judged unfairly based on my background, I didn't let those experiences ultimately define me.

Two years later, when I resigned from my position as treasurer, I was invited to a private farewell with President Bush. I felt honored that the president acknowledged the end of my service. My family was invited and since my dad was visiting me in Virginia, I asked him to come along. The scene that would materialize later is one that will forever be imprinted in my mind.

I brought my dad into the Oval Office and he and President Bush exchanged pleasantries. The president then turned to my dad and—in the most genuine manner—thanked my dad for his daughter's service to this nation. The president of one of the most powerful countries of the world was thanking my father, a janitor. It was clear that my grandma Juanita might as well have raised the president; he was leading by example in treating everyone with respect.

A Lesson in Customer Service

One of the first jobs I had was as a customer service representative for the towel company Barth & Dreyfus. I quickly learned that the customer is always right. I also became adept at handling difficult customers. There was this specific client who everyone in the department avoided because he had a reputation for being impossible to please. Since I was the new girl on the block, I was granted the privilege of taking his call. I had no idea that he had such a reputation when we spoke, but I handled him the same way I would any other customer. He was so impressed with my manners that he asked to speak with the vice president of our company. It must have been glowing praise because I was promptly put in charge of the three biggest chains we handled.

I literally took that lesson to the bank and then into my political career. It was clear that if you treat everyone with courtesy and respect—regardless of who they are—then you will become a valuable asset to your company. You may not know who the person on the other end of the line is; it could be that she is related to your boss, or some future client. The bottom line is that if you treat everyone with respect, you can never go wrong.

It reminds me of the old saying: "Be very nice to the people on your way up because you may see them on your way down." I have always treated interns as if they will one day be my bosses. As a matter of fact, I know some big shots in President George W. Bush's administration who started as interns with him when he was the governor of Texas or in his father's administration.

On the other hand, I would never expect special treatment from anyone based on positions I have held. That means I'll never ask someone to do something that I'd be unwilling to do myself. I know I have come across many people who feel as though they only have to be kind to people in positions of power or from a higher economic status. It could become tricky for people who, whether consciously or subconsciously, look for signs of people's status before they decide on how they should be treated. People don't necessarily carry around name tags with such information.

This reminds me of what happened to a friend of mine who was a local restaurant owner. Out of his eleven brothers, he counted himself among the nine who owned restaurants. It had long been a dream of his to buy a luxury car like a Lexus or a Cadillac, but he found it hard to justify spending that much. He also didn't want to get into a long-term payment plan. He decided that he would start setting aside small amounts of money over the years and then one day pay for it in full. After many years, he finally had enough saved up. He left work that day with a mission: to pull into his driveway that night with a new luxury car. He didn't have time to go home and change, so he showed up in his regular work clothes—apparel appropriate for cooking, cleaning, and washing dishes.

When he arrived at the sales lot, he began to meander along the rows of cars in search of his dream car. He didn't know what he was looking for, only that he'd know it when he saw it. And then, he saw it and knew that car would be his. A salesman approached him—as he was admiring his dream car—and asked him if he needed any help. My friend patted the hood of the car he imagined soon to be his and said, "That's it, that's the one." The salesman suggested they take a walk around the lot to see if there was anything else that interested my friend. My friend, undeterred, kept asking about the original car, and the salesman finally paused and said, "You can't afford it."

Frustrated, my friend asked to speak to the manager.

When the manager came, my friend told him that he had been saving up to buy a car for years, and that he was a local restaurant owner who had been prepared to buy the car right then and there. Unfortunately, his salesperson had insulted him. He informed the manager that he was going to go to another lot that same day and buy the very same car that had been denied him. My friend looked back as he walked away and saw the manager berating his employee.

Every time someone compliments my friend's car, he tells this story. I think it's a story worth telling.

4. Listen to Yourself.

As you begin to discover your purpose in life, there will be many people telling you what *they* think you should do. Most of the time people mean well and you should at least listen to different points of view. As a matter of fact, you should encourage different perspectives and approaches. Consider yourself lucky that people care enough about you to offer their opinions. Be sure to remain calm and simply listen, ask questions, and imagine yourself in different scenarios.

After this information-gathering stage, it's time to take a step back and listen to your inner voice. After you have exhausted all possible outlets for information, it is this voice that you should pay the closest attention to. Sometimes you may not like what it has to say, but trust it. There are many names for this inner voice. Some call it conscience, others a gut feeling, and then there's the concept of having a soul.

Whatever you label it, this is a part of yourself that you must master connecting with. You must learn to separate this voice from all of the other conflicting messages that are constantly bombarding you on any given day. If for whatever reason you begin to silence this voice, it will eventually stop speaking.

Running for City Council

I had never run for public office and thought it best to seek the advice of my most trusted friends: Jim McDowall, an older gentleman who became my friend while I was in Sacramento and serving on the State Council on Developmental Disabilities; Mr. Kyman, my former boss from City National Bank; and Jorge Azpiazu, a friend I had made when I complained about a commercial his company was running that I found insensitive to families that had children with disabilities. They offered different perspectives, but all agreed that it was a good opportunity for me to pursue. It may be a lot of work, but if anyone could do it, I could.

In the end, it was my voice that I needed to listen to. It proudly confirmed what my advisors thought. I was confident that this would be the right thing to do for my family, children, and community. Seeking this elected position would be the continuation of my mission in life. It was important for me to consult with as many of my friends and family members as I could before taking the plunge. Not everyone I spoke with was excited for me. My mother, especially, was concerned about my entering politics because she had heard it could be a nasty arena: the scrutiny, the lies, the soiled reputations. She was concerned about my safety and the safety of my children. I tried to assuage her fears, but she was still reluctant. I knew from prior elections that local politics could get personal and that she was right to be concerned. My opponents could paint such an ugly picture of me that my family wouldn't even recognize me. I had to remember that she was my mother and her advice came from love. As well intentioned as people can be, always take into account the role they play in your life and what's at stake for them in your decision. In the case of my mom, she was looking out for my best interests, but there are many who may give you advice based on selfish interests. Always take into account the sender of the message in order to know how to best receive it.

Becoming Treasurer of the United States

Whether to move forward with becoming the forty-first treasurer of the United States was one of the most important decisions I would ever have to make. Unlike past experiences, I was not allowed to take a survey as to how to best proceed. I was only allowed to speak with my family; I'd be asking them to pay a hefty price by uprooting our life to move to D.C. I knew that this decision would have historical importance, as I'd be the first immigrant to hold this office. I'd be representative of not only the local immigrant community, but also Latinos throughout the country. I was not going to take this position if I could not fulfill it to the best of my abilities. Now more than ever, I had to rely on my inner voice.

As with other positions I have held, this one came to me. I did not seek it out, although some might believe I did because I was such an advocate in the Bush campaign. Looking back over my career, I can't help but feel like many

234 | *Rosario Marín*

of these opportunities were preordained. Events happened to fall into place and too many coincidences came to pass that I refused to believe that my life was spreading out before me in an arbitrary manner. I believe in God—but even if you don't, it helps to believe in a higher power. Despite your religious affiliation, you should, most importantly, believe in yourself. In this situation, I listened to two entities: God and myself. Both were saying that yes, I should pursue this opportunity. I knew that if it were meant to be, the universe and God would provide the resources and guidance I'd need to continue my life's mission. Events in the appointing process went smoothly. As treasurer, I was able to work on issues and campaigns that were meaningful to the Latino community and me. Once again, my inner voice had not failed me.

Running for the U.S. Senate

This decision would be another life-changing experience; just considering it was energy draining. I had moved my family three thousand miles away to D.C., my husband had just secured a permanent job at HUD, the kids loved their schools—Eric was especially thriving in his high school. We had fallen into a great family routine. Many would not have even considered such an idea.

I began the survey process of talking with people whose judgment I trusted. Shirley Wheat, my chief of staff, had always been a pragmatic individual willing to lend an ear. She said that she could see me as a senator; as such I could have greater influence over important decisions. Her opinion weighed heavily in my decision because of the great amount of respect I held for her. She was my first stop on a select list of people I needed to speak with.

I continued by contacting Marty Linsky, my trusted advisor and professor from the Kennedy School of Government at Harvard University. We met in New York where he resides. He was excited about the possibility and said that he could only see positive results. If I won the primary and then the general election, it would be historic. But, even if I lost either, I would still make history as the first immigrant Latina to run for Senate. I did not take his words lightly since he had always been right on the money and I had come to respect all of his advice. I concurred with his assessment that history would be made regardless. Of course, it would be preferable for me to win the seat.

I contacted Mr. Kyman, the former president of the bank. I had turned to him for advice over the years and he had always been honest in his assessment. Over a tasty lunch in Orange County, he basically said that there were only positive results to be gained from making the attempt. He acknowledged that it was most likely going to be a tough race, but well worth the effort.

I contacted Governor Pete Wilson by phone. He had been a U.S. senator before he was elected governor.

"Do you know what it will take?" he asked.

I answered his question with another: "Besides the twenty million dollars?"

"Well, yes, that about covers it," he said.

He then went on to say that my opponent was formidable, but that I had what it took to be a serious candidate. He is a clever politician and certainly the only Republican to have won statewide office several times in recent history. If anyone knew the political landscape, he did. He paused and said that it would be a difficult campaign, but certainly feasible. I asked if he'd support me and he said that, as a former governor, he'd have to follow the tradition of staying out of the primary. If I should be successful in the primary, however, he'd lend his support. I tried to convince him that I was the best candidate and that no one stood a better chance should I seek the nomination. He agreed but would not endorse me or anyone else. He wished me a lot of luck because, having been through a Senate race himself, he knew I would need it. I thanked him. I felt that while I had not been successful in securing his support, I had his promise to stay out of the primary race, which assured a level playing field.

I remember my first meeting with Ken Khachigian, the brilliant political consultant who was a speechwriter for Ronald Reagan. He was beyond well connected in the political world and his ear was always glued to the ground. There is no political move that he has not anticipated or political game he doesn't understand. He's a wonderful listener who carefully prods, questions, and challenges. When our long conversation was winding down, he said: "I've met with a lot of people who want to run for Senate and I believe you can make it. There is no one in this world who wants to beat Boxer more than I do, and I believe that you may just have a chance at it." He informed me that the moment Boxer thought I was going to run, she'd go right after me. I anticipated a long drawn-out fight, but with Ken by my side, I'd be fine. He had the wisdom that comes from experience. I was eager to be taken under his wing. The security he provided me with is something I will forever be grateful for.

Clearly I had the input of my most trusted friends, my family, and Ken, who would become my campaign advisor. I had gone through the rituals of my decision-making process and felt that I had carefully weighed the advantages against the disadvantages. Like in every other decision, however, the voice that I ultimately listened to was my own. I knew that pursuing this position was something that I had to do. Having checked with myself, I could be satisfied with whatever the outcome would be.

5. Choose Carefully and Then Act.

When facing a number of choices, you must consider the consequences of each one. You should invite conflicting arguments from people you trust. Take everything into account as you map out the different paths you could potentially walk down. Analyze, analyze, analyze, and then, once you feel you are ready, act swiftly with the confidence of a decision well made.

Power Is Only Good If You Can Walk Away from It

I can still vividly recall how many people were crying during the final celebrations when the governor's term came to an end due to term limits. We had been in power for eight years and soon we'd no longer be there. I had served in various capacities for seven of those years and I knew that I'd miss the people I worked with. I did not, however, have any concerns about being out of a job or no longer being in power.

I was at peace, having had the rewarding opportunity to help govern a great state; I knew that it was now someone else's turn. I could walk away without resentment or regret, and I was filled with pride in my own professional accomplishments. I had done everything that I could have done. There was not one more letter I could have written, one more phone call I could have made, one more report that I could have given.

I was the last person to leave the Los Angeles governor's office, and I flicked off the lights on December 31, 1999. It was almost six o'clock and the office was ready for the new governor's team to come in two days later. I walked away with my head up high and never turned back. That was the day I realized what it meant to walk away from power. It became sparklingly clear to me that the power had never been mine to begin with; it was simply loaned to me. Citizens had given me the ability to create positive change through electing the governor, but the power truly belonged to them. I wish I could write a whole separate book on this very topic and give it to everyone in public service. Why? Because when you learn to walk away from power, the decisions you make will become easier and your choices will be clear.

People give you power for a limited amount of time and they can certainly take it away. You can hold it for a while, but, as with anything that is lent to you, you must return it. The public can choose to give you or someone else power at their will. So do the best that you can while you have it and never forget that it is not yours. Make people proud that they gave you the privilege to hold it for a period of time but prepare yourself to give it back at a moment's notice. This deep understanding of power can be both humbling and liberating. The more power that has been entrusted to you, the more humble you should become. It is a great privilege to hold power, but if you can't walk away from it, then it isn't worth having. It is in these cases that you no longer possess power, but it still possesses you.

So, what to do? Hit the ground running. No matter which position I have held or which position I will one day hold, I know that my time is limited. To be effective, I make sure I develop an agenda right away. Whether it is going to be two or ten years—I know the clock is ticking. I make sure to ask myself the relevant questions: What is the history of this office? What is truly the important work of this office? How is it being accomplished? What priorities are being worked on? And what needs to be done to expedite success? Just as important, I need to find out immediately what the biggest problems confronting us are and what we can do to remedy the situation. What is it that I really want to accomplish in this position? How will I want to be remembered when I leave? What are my own priorities?

One thing that has become clear to me is that regardless of the previous person's priorities, she is no longer there. By the same token, when I leave and my replacement arrives, she will come with her own priorities. Thus, I must leave something behind. The sooner I'm able to articulate what my goals are, the greater the chances that they'll be realized.

I was able to once again walk away from power to head into the unknown when I decided to leave my comfortable position as mayor and council member in Huntington Park to venture into the unknown territory of the federal government. Being asked to serve as treasurer was certainly a coveted opportunity, but it came with uncertainty and possible failure. What if things didn't work out in D.C. after I had already given up my elected position? Could I walk away from the security I had as a council member and not regret it later if things didn't work out? I had already been on the council for seven years, and there were no term limits. One of my colleagues had been on the council for almost thirty years. Elective office had treated me well and I had achieved some remarkable successes for our city. It was precisely those successes that had brought me to the attention of President Bush.

I was so busy representing the significant needs of my community within organizations such as the League of California Cities, the Latino Caucus, the National Association of Latino Elected and Appointed Officials, and others that leaving the council was a difficult decision to make. I had humbly achieved an important level of recognition. I was at a high point in my career and had enough influence to enact real change. To leave all that I was comfortable with to venture into Washington—where I knew nobody and would have much less influence—was a consideration in the back of my mind. Yes, it would be a history-making opportunity, but what if I failed? Would it simply be a historical failure? What if I lost all that I had worked so hard to achieve?

I examined my accomplishments and asked myself whether I had done everything I could've as a council member and mayor. I could honestly say that I was content with how much effort I had put into my positions. As mayor, I was confident that I had worked harder than any previous person in that position because I dedicated 100 percent of my time. Former mayors had only devoted a part of their time to their council duties because they were usually business-people who attended to their businesses first.

As mayor, it was important for me to accomplish as much as I could because I saw that many of the city's needs had not been satisfied. I had set out to accomplish several concrete tasks as mayor and I had succeeded. I had a clear track record of accomplishments and could proudly say that I had completed more than anyone had anticipated. I took it as a sign that my community approved of my performance when I was reelected. Certainly there was more to be done and I could continue in my position for a long time, or I could be satisfied with a job well done and pass my power down to someone else.

As far as I was concerned, if I were going to Washington, it would be to be the best treasurer I could and to make my community even more proud of me. I had to ask myself if I could've honestly done more with the time I had as council member. Was there something I was leaving undone for the next mayor? Had I lived up to my promises? These were among my considerations. In the end, I found solace know-ing that I had done everything I could with the power that my community had granted me. I could look them in the eye and say thank you.

In leaving my position as mayor to become treasurer, I was filled with the same feeling of accomplishment that had accompanied my former decision to leave the governor's office. Then came the time to consider walking out of the treasurer's office to run for a seat in the Senate. I went through a similar decision-making process of sizing up my accomplishments and asking myself—in this case—if I could walk away from the highest office I had ever held in my political career. I had almost completed two years as treasurer and was highly involved in a number of duties, from financial literacy efforts in the Hispanic community to being a part of the president's economic recovery team. The press and others seemed to be noticing my significant accomplishments. One of my staff members who had worked under a number of U.S. treasurers often told reporters that I had been the best treasurer she had ever worked for. Knowing full well that things might not turn out as I envisioned, I decided to take the risk by leaving my assured position to embark on an uncertain Senate race.

When word got out that I was resigning from my treasurer position, many questioned my sanity. How could I give up such a safe, secure, and distinguished position for a series of . . . maybes? Sure, there was a significant risk in this new endeavor, and clearly no political campaign is a shoo-in, especially considering this would be my first statewide run. Why didn't I just stay put as the treasurer of the United States—a position I could potentially hold for a total of seven years if the president was reelected? Why would I give up that security? These were all questions I answered before moving forward. And, even knowing all the potential downsides, I decided to go for it. Many reminded me of the old saying that "a bird in the hand is worth two in the bush." But I'd counter with the question that had always clarified my decisions in such moments: What good is power if I cannot walk away from it? It is an uncomfortable question for many to answer because they realize the impurity of their intentions. Of course I could stay comfortably nestled in my current position—or I could try to become the first Latina U.S. senator. A Senate position would give me the ability to have a greater impact on the lives of the people I'd represent. In addition, in the process of campaigning for the Senate, I'd be the only Latina running in the entire country and could help the president's relection by connecting with minorities and women's groups. My campaign would attract national attention.

Yes, there was much to lose, but even greater things to be gained if I was successful. Although the public perception of people in appointed positions is that they wield a lot of power, the actuality is that the people are the ones with the true power. In my case, any power I thought I had was fleeting and granted to me through the president who had been elected by the majority of the people. My true power would lie in being able to walk away from my position with the hope that I'd be able to accomplish even more good as a senator. I made sure that no matter how passionate I was about politics, no matter how honored I was to be the treasurer, I would never allow a title—no matter how high ranking—to define me. I was also confident that I did not need a certain title to grant me happiness. Whatever power or authority you think you may own, remember that it's only an illusion and one you can certainly walk away from if it is for a potentially greater opportunity. For me, the thought of leaving what many people would do anything to keep actually gave me a sense of empowerment because I was certain that I was doing it for the right reasons.

I resigned from my position as treasurer with a sense of peace. I had worked 24/7, didn't take vacations, and took countless business trips across the U.S. I fulfilled my position with dignity and grace, and I could walk away with my head held high.

Painful but Not Difficult Decisions

I learned a good deal from working with Governor Wilson that has helped me to this day. He used to say that there are decisions that may be painful to make, but they are not difficult. Now whenever I hesitate before a difficult decision, I ask myself why: Is it because it is truly a difficult decision with many factors to consider? Or because it is simply a decision whose results may be painful? Asking myself these questions is helpful in creating an objectivity that I may lack initially. Often, it gives me a sense of how to best proceed with a clear sense of direction. It doesn't allow me to procrastinate, because when I look at the cold facts (however difficult), more often than not I see that what I am facing only seems like a challenging decision because it will be painful to execute. The sooner you can learn how to make this distinction, the better, because you can focus on making your way through the pain instead of being muddled by your thoughts.

One of the most vivid examples I can recall of this problem is when the chief of police of my city asked me to consider changing the laws so that he could purchase his dream house that happened to lie twenty-five miles outside of the established boundaries. When he came to talk with me, I felt conflicted because we all knew that he was the best chief that our city had ever had the luck of employing. The police department was running like a well-oiled machine, with morale at an all-time high. The community respected and admired him. Normally, such a request would not even be entertained, but given how much he had given to his position over the years, I was torn. The original intent of the law when it had been established many years ago was to make sure that the chief of police would be able to respond to an emergency within a reasonable amount of time. However, I thought, in this day of advanced communications, in most cases the need to have someone in person had been reduced.

The chief was eloquent in providing a compelling argument for why we should change the law. He explained that he'd have the ability to communicate directly with the people on the ground in case of an emergency. He even made it known that the house was so important to his wife that if they weren't able to purchase it, he might have to find another city where he could serve as chief.

I listened carefully to the chief, but I knew that I had to put my respect for him aside and put the needs of my community ahead of all else. The real question was whether the original intent of the law was still a valid one. In all honesty, I would have to say yes. How could we, as a council, discount the validity of the law when, if there were a true emergency, the chief could possibly be missing from action? Also, how could I justify such a bending of the rules to the other members of the administration who had to live within the established boundaries? Or, to appease everyone, would we have to make a sweeping change that would cover all of the affected employees? Where would it stop? We certainly couldn't change the law for just one individual, no matter how valuable he was. And what about the future? What if another chief wanted to live one hundred miles away?

After all of these considerations, it was not a difficult

decision for me to make, but it was a painful one. I considered the chief a friend and I had a good relationship with his wife; I sympathized with his family situation. I knew that if I refused to go forward with changing the law, then there was the real possibility of losing him. I called the chief to let him know of my decision and everything I had considered. I made it clear that this was nothing personal, but only the right decision to make for the city. I acknowledged how valuable he was to the city, but there was nothing else I could do. The chief listened carefully and acknowledged that he was putting the council in a bind. He appreciated the fast turnaround on the decision and said he'd do his best to find a home that was closer. Luckily he was able to find another home within the boundaries and he continued to serve as the chief of police. I had stood my ground. A line had been drawn and I still count the chief as one of my dear friends.

One of the things that I usually do when making a decision is to take people's names out of the equation. Good public policy should never be based on a particular individual. There have been countless times when I've seen leaders in both the political and business worlds make important decisions or set policies based on a particular individual. When the individual leaves, they are left to deal with the consequences of their decision that was made with specific names attached to it. Better to eliminate the names from the beginning to avoid future conflict. A good policy is exactly that and should be able to stand the test of time and change of personnel.

One of the goals of good policy making is to ensure that its development is transparent and that the resulting policy is transferable. If this is the case, the policy will stand regardless of changing circumstances. Looking back, I know that it would have been less painful for me to change the law for the chief, and, most likely, it would not have been difficult to justify such a decision. A good chief of police does not come along every day and we could've spun the decision as a necessity to keep him on staff. At the end of the day, I would've had to live with a poorly made decision. It was not difficult for me to maintain the integrity of the law that had been established for the safety of our community, but it certainly had the potential to be painful.

Make Your Decision and Don't Look Back . . . At Least Not with Regret!

In almost all cases, indecision breeds confusion, fear, doubts, and (at its worst) resentment. The roles I have held required that I make hundreds of decisions. When there is an assembly line's worth of decisions to make, there is simply no time for indecision. The perfect decision rarely exists, but if you have gathered as many facts and opinions as possible before making a decision, you will certainly be in an ideal position to take action. Governor Wilson used to say that the perfect law did not exist, and therefore we must make sure to reduce the negative consequences of any proposed legislation. You should do the same. Once your decision is ready to be made, prepare yourself to diminish any of the resulting negative consequences. If you are in charge of a team or if your decision will affect many people, it's best if you clearly outline your decision-making process to them. This transparency has helped me tremendously with my staff. They have been able to see how my mind thinks through decisions and have (hopefully) seen the level of consideration I deem appropriate.

What's most important is that once you've made a firm decision, you move forward with confidence in your abilities. If you have successfully taken into account all factors (without dwelling too long on needless distractions), then you'll feel the urge to take purposeful action. Don't second-guess yourself. I have never seen anyone use second-guessing as a viable decision-making strategy.

After I lost the U.S. Senate run (due to unanticipated events), many people asked if I regretted leaving my position as treasurer. I could honestly say no because I had run through my entire decision-making process with the information that was available to me at the time. There was peace in my heart and mind. I had evaluated potential outcomes and, of course, losing was one of those potential outcomes. Simply because events did not turn out the way I would've hoped does not mean that it was the wrong decision for me to have made. I have no regrets.

Of course, hindsight is 20/20 and there was no way that I could've predicted the events that would unfold after my decision had already been made. The recall election in California qualified for the ballot and Arnold Schwarzenegger put his name in the hat at the last minute. Not only did he win, but he also endorsed my opponent. If these events were a part of my initial information-gathering process, then the resulting decision would not have been the same: I would not have left my position as treasurer. You make the best decision possible with what you know for certain. Spending time on unpredictable what-ifs is certainly a waste of energy. In my opinion, time is always ticking and therefore it is of the highest value. Better to keep marching forward than backward. Although not every decision will necessarily lead to success, it does not mean that failure is the only other result. What's of the most importance is that you don't look back, because before you know it, the next decision—which could potentially alter your life—may need to be made.

6. As Hard As It May Be, Fake Courage.

There will be times when you feel like you cannot face the world. You will go through experiences that have the potential to devastate your life. It is during these times that you must dig deep and summon the will to rise in the morning and face your opponents, yourself, and the world. Confront the challenge as an opportunity to show courage and if it feels like you are an actor faking fortitude and courage in a bad melodrama, then that is just fine. Those who are close to you will most likely recognize that all is not well, but they will marvel at your strength in trying to be strong. And, those who don't know you will not be able to tell the difference between "fake" and real courage. From the outside, the two almost look identical. If you fake it long enough, you'll realize soon enough that it begins to feel real. Eventually you, too, will not be able to tell the difference.

On one of the worst days of my life, my friend Jim sent me a warm letter with a quotation from Theodore Roosevelt that read:

"It is not the critic who counts: not the man who points out how the strong man stumbles or where the doer of deeds could

have done better. The credit belongs to the man who is actually in the arena, whose face is marred by dust and sweat and blood, who strives valiantly, who errs and comes up short again and again, because there is no effort without error or shortcoming, but who knows the great enthusiasms, the great devotions, who spends himself for a worthy cause; who, at the best, knows, in the end, the triumph of high achievement, and who, at the worst, if he fails, at least he fails while daring greatly, so that his place shall never be with those cold and timid souls who knew neither victory nor defeat."

I cut that block of text from the letter and carried it around with me. After reading it over so many times I could almost recite it verbatim. What's more important is that I internalized it so completely that I no longer needed a scrap of paper to remind me of its importance. That quote and the creed from the Special Olympics have acted as mantras in my life. The creed is simple and its essence mirrors Roosevelt's: "Let me win, but if I cannot win let me be brave in the attempt." In ancient Rome, the gladiators went into the arena with this credo. If it was strong enough to pull them through their great physical challenges, then one would hope it could help us as well.

More than thirty years ago, Eunice Kennedy Shriver created the Special Olympics with the absolute conviction that people with intellectual disabilities could practice sports if we took the time to teach and train them; they could utilize the power of sports to lead productive lives. The credo every Special Olympics athlete recites has helped me through some difficult times and has always clarified what separates effective leaders from others is how they choose to face the difficult times in their lives. In my view the divide occurs in their sense of courage—a quality that separates the weak from the strong and the mediocre from the daring. All this is not to suggest that acting courageously is easy. On the contrary, courage is not easily won.

There have been many times both politically and personally where life and its challenges seemed overwhelming. These were times where I was scared, tired, upset, distraught—and yet I found the fortitude to make my way through painful events. Most people who surrounded me during these difficult times would never know what I was feeling. I made sure that time after time I entered that arena even if it was at a great emotional expense. I contented myself with knowing that I'd look back with satisfaction on how I handled various situations: I didn't give in and I wouldn't give up. I suggest you do the same. Regardless of who your opponents may be, never fear entering the arena even if it means you must fake courage. Make sure that your larger objective is strong enough to sustain you.

What's magical about courage is that it is not important that you feel it, but that your actions confirm it to the outside world. In my life, it has been best boiled down to one eloquent sentence delivered when I needed it the most by a friend: "Don't let the bastards take the best of you; don't let them see you cry."

Lights, Camera, and Faking Courage

It's always a strange experience when you first see yourself framed within a television screen or hear your voice through a recorder. You recognize what you see and hear as both you and not you. For a few minutes you imagine that this must be how the world sees you. This leads to some serious cringing but, in time, it also leads to some revelations. After seeing myself on the news after political disappointments, I came to the realization that to the public (and to myself watching myself), there was no difference between the physical manifestation of real or fake courage.

If you can hold back the tears, anger, and vacillation and instead convey confidence, you'll come through successfully. No one will know the difference. When you successfully convey courage, you'll become courageous in the eyes of others, and their resulting confidence in you will give you strength. This has happened to me on several occasions, but the moment that immediately comes to mind is when I was facing the death of my Senate campaign. Although it was a very difficult test for me to endure, I did, and no one could see that I was dying on the inside. Several television stations looped my speech and each time I saw it, I marveled at how I was able to pull it off. Although I'm a firm believer that the prayers of friends and family helped, in the end, it was just the cameras and me. Everyone, including myself, saw a calm and composed candidate who, no matter how hard she had tried, would not make it past the primary.

Gun to My Head

I was often busy running around and, as a result, one day I forgot an important document that I needed for a meeting. My watch said it was almost two in the afternoon and the meeting was to occur in a few minutes. Luckily, I didn't live far away; I decided to get into my little Miata and zip home to retrieve the forgotten document. Like others do, I decided I'd return a few phone calls in the car during a route that I could practically navigate with my eyes closed. Pulling into my driveway, I hit the garage door opener button and slid my car in. I shut off the car's engine and tried to bring the conversation I was having to a close when, glancing into my rearview mirror, I saw a young man with a shaved head. He swaggered into my garage dressed in an oversized T-shirt, crumpled khakis, and tennis shoes.

All I could think to do was repeat "Oh my God!" into my cell phone. Before I knew it, a royal blue and silver gun that resembled a toy was aimed at my head. I didn't see my life flash before me like is popularly believed, but I did see the faces of my three children floating around me.

"Give me your purse and phone," he said.

My breathing quickened and I tried my best to fake courage and not freeze completely. I was a prisoner in my own car. So, this is how it all ends, I thought. I readily complied with his commands and looked at him straight in the eye as I handed over my possessions.

"Don't look at me!" he said.

It was too late: this man's face with its dark brown anger-infused eyes and bushy eyebrows permanently imprinted itself in my mind's eye. He ran away, becoming a drifting figure in my rearview mirror that would haunt me for years to come.

Although I was really shaken, I ran inside the house and called the police. A few moments later, I saw the familiar face of Officer Luna and completely broke down—I was shattered. I asked him how this could happen in broad daylight; it wasn't as though I had been confronted in a dark alley at three in the morning. How brazen were gang members getting that they were assaulting people right outside of their own homes? How could one of them assault me? As a councilwoman, I represented the people and had oversight of the police department. Then I realized that I had just had a representative experience of what life was like in my city. I wanted to believe that the attack was random, but later events would prove that theory doubtful. What caused me further distress was seeing how young my assailant was—it was clear that gangs had a greater influence and power than I had wanted to acknowledge. This was a deeply rooted problem. The whole experience was a sad and embarrassing commentary on the quality of life in my city.

Now more than ever, I was resolute in my need to eliminate the city of its gang problem: I wanted them out for good. I hated what they had done to our sense of safety, our business community, and our young people. Gangs had dramatically brought down the standard of living in a once proud city. They were taking over bit by bit like a deadly virus. The gang member who assaulted me didn't just take away my purse and cell phone; he robbed me of any peace of mind that I once had. I could replace my possessions, but my psyche had taken a serious beating; I could extrapolate the effects the attack had on me to what the city was experiencing as a whole.

Many nights followed with my sleeping in the fetal position, my husband scratching my back to calm me. He worried about me and suggested that I take a vacation to Mexico to have some time away for myself and away from the city. I tried to shake the experience off, but it held on tightly like a diabolical monkey on my back. My mind was probably my own worst enemy, projecting the terrifying images of the event inside the walls of my skull, replaying them like a looped horror film that I couldn't escape. Whenever I pulled into the garage, I felt the gang member's presence. I was constantly looking in the frame of my rearview mirror— afraid to move ahead with my life. With time, the trauma of the event would lose its razor edge, but never fade away completely. I had been seriously violated for the second time in my life, but this time I was not a child. I was an adult in a position to do something about it.

Faking the Courage

I had a deeply seated unease until we sold that house. I still, occasionally, feel an indescribable paranoia and resist the urge to look in my rearview mirror. I fear seeing those angry eyes highlighted by their bushy eyebrows.

I did go to Mexico, and when I returned decided to fight not only my insecurities, but also the city's pervading gang problem. It was us against them and we were losing against their arsenal of drugs, alcohol, prostitution, and drive-by shootings. Part of the council's efforts included bringing in the new chief of police. The council promised that we would somehow give him all the resources he needed to make a tangible difference in the community. Our objective was clear: to rid the city of gangs and watch the soaring crime rate descend. We knew it would be an uphill battle—so the sooner we got to climbing, the better. We had to deal with the by-product of gangs fighting among themselves for territory: the mourning of families with deceased gang members.

I became as personally involved in the effort as possible,

often cruising with police officers through the city's streets. It was my philosophy that I would never ask someone to do something I was unwilling to do—and that included fighting crime. If I asked the police officers to patrol the streets at two in the morning, then I should be willing to ride along with them. Although I would not, of course, be able to do anything hands-on, I would not turn away from the problem; it would be something that I would witness with my own eyes. I made sure to stop by the police department during Christmas, New Year's, and other holidays because if they were willing to give up time with their families, then I should do the same. I felt strongly that if they were there with the mission of protecting our city, to make sure that we could enjoy our holidays, then the least that I could do was show my support.

During these ride-alongs with the police, I came to a deeper understanding of the psychological and sociological forces that intermingle to bring about gang violence. I'll never forget one morning around two A.M. when we heard nearby gunshots. It was difficult to discern where the alarming sounds originated, but the officer called dispatch and immediately rushed to where his instincts pointed. The whole procedure happened with swift movements and a rapidity that could only come from experience. Within minutes I saw another scene that would never leave me: an eleven-year-old boy in the bed of a pickup truck with blood dripping from a wound in his back. His older brother cradled him and kept on repeating, "No, no. Not my little brother, please not my little brother." He looked up at us in tears and explained that a car had driven by and one of the men had asked him where he was from and he replied, "Nowhere." Evidently this was the wrong answer. Several random shots were unleashed and one hit his brother.

Although I was supposed to stay out of the way, my motherly instincts took over and I rushed to the young boy in the back of the truck. I had gotten close enough to see the wound and his pale face before the officers held me back. So many questions immediately came to mind, the first being the obvious: What is such a young boy doing out at two in the morning? Where are his parents? Lowering the incidence of gang violence was already a personal matter for me, but seeing this boy bleeding profusely gave me the sheer determination to make sure that these senseless crimes stopped. The crimes, unfortunately, continued. Soon after, there was another drive-by shooting that claimed the life of a young girl. The investigation led to the shooter, who would end up being shot himself, by one his own gang members for bringing too much attention upon the gang. That shooter also ended up in jail. In the end, three families would forever be altered because of one meaningless crime. I saw firsthand that the only thing more painful than giving birth to a child was burying that same child. My heart went out to all of the suffering mothers—the girl's mother especially, because there was nothing she could have done to protect her daughter from something as unpredictable as a drive-by shooting. I also felt sorry for the other two mothers because they had not given birth to killers: something in between their births and deaths had gone horribly wrong. I wondered if there was something more those two mothers could have done. Their two sons grew up surrounded by crime and they, perhaps, thought if they couldn't

beat the gangs, then they'd join them. They learned to sur-
vive. Of course, they had to take personal responsibility, but
that seemed not to matter much when I saw the havoc that
their deaths had on those they left behind.

We did everything we could to clean up our community.
We held monthly vigils, and brought the governor, the
district attorney, and the California attorney general to our
city. The results started to show in lowered crime rates.
Meanwhile, we were also dealing with the serious problem
of the selling of illegal documents to undocumented workers. These particular operations threatened to completely
overtake Pacific Boulevard, which ran through the heart of
our business district. People couldn't walk a block without
being harassed by at least several dealers trying to sell illegal
driver's licenses, Social Security numbers, and green cards. I
was walking with the chief of police (dressed in street
clothes) and several colleagues one day when a man trying to
sell documents approached us.

I had had enough! When we got back to the police station, I expressed the need to clean up the business district of
the *miqueros* (people who sell false documents). I was the
most outspoken council member on this particular issue, and
before long, a task force was created that had an obvious
effect. This upset some people. Several weeks later, a business acquaintance of mine advised me to stop my efforts to
rid the boulevard of the *miqueros*. She told me that she was
simply relaying the message that had been given to her.
They told her that I was hurting "their business." She
seemed genuinely concerned for my well-being. I thanked
her for the message and told her that she could tell them that

no amount of intimidation would stop our efforts and that they were not welcome in our city. The legitimate businesses were the ones taking the most severe blows from the hostile business environment that these document peddlers were creating in the district. As they expected. I was shaken by this warning—but I made sure to deliver my message with a deliberate confidence that I wasn't truly feeling.

Alarmed, I visited the chief of police and told him about the ominous warning. We decided that although we would proceed with all of our plans, I'd stop being the media front person for a while. I did exactly that, but the *miqueros* were determined to get their message across. I was soon being stalked. At first I was in denial, thinking that it was just paranoia, but it soon became clear that I was, indeed, being followed both on foot and by car. One time, I called the police and they told me not to go into my house. I went around and around my block before the police showed up and suggested I alternate my routes home to avoid becoming even more of a target. Soon surveillance was set up around my house and a police car accompanied me home each night after the city council meetings. It took months of raids that resulted in many going to jail or back to their home countries before the business district was cleaned up.

Although the *miqueros* attempted to use intimidation to curtail our efforts, we persevered and were rewarded. There were many times when I trembled as I walked home and was scared for my life, but the public face I lent to the fight was always one of strength. The crime problem was more important than my fears. Of course, it would have certainly been easier and safer to ignore the problem, but that is why it had gotten so bad in the first place. What kind of public servant would I have been if I ignored the serious problems my city was facing? I learned long ago that *"el valiente vive hasta que el cobarde quiere"* (the strongman lives only as long as the coward lets him). The gangs would succeed until the community rose up against them. We did and the gangs had no choice but to find another place to go. We made it clear that they were no longer running the show in Huntington Park. Regardless of whether I sometimes relied on fake courage to get me through, the result of a safer city was worth the effort.

7. When You Attain Power, Be Sure to Use It.

If you follow the six previous actions in this chapter and couple them with hard work, you will almost certainly find yourself in a position of power. In that case, this final mandate that brings us to the end of our journey together is particularly important. Power and influence are relative and exist in personal, business, political, and other settings. What's most important is that once you attain the position you have sought, you make sure to exercise the power you now possess. You have walked a long path and to not use your influence for good would mean your efforts will be in vain. I have seen corrupt power, but I've also seen how it can be used wisely and with purpose. For instance, using your power to eliminate barriers that could impede others from following in your footsteps is something worth striving for. Seeing others achieve success because you helped, rather than hindered, is a great reward.

The world needs more leaders who accomplish both good and great deeds. These leaders come in all shapes and sizes and from different facets of society. Will you be one of those leaders? Will you rise to the occasion? In my life, working in government is where I happened to find the most opportunities to use my power for good. Whatever segment of society you may find yourself in, you'll be a much happier person if you've used your power to create a better world. Some believe that this philosophy is unrealistic in a harsh business environment where competition is often cut-throat, or in whatever other setting where there are many shortcuts to attaining power. The truth is that these short-cuts only lead to an illusion of power. True influence is hard earned and well worth the effort. The better you understand the different dimensions of power, the better prepared you will be for the journey that lies ahead.

Power Can Be Corruptive

It was a learning experience to see how one of my colleagues who had been on the council for a long time used his power to help his friends. Although I'd seen many examples in the news and elsewhere of how politics can be corrupt, that was no substitute for seeing it firsthand. I remember one particular day when a contract was taken away from a vendor— through no fault of its own—and given to this councilman's friend. The friend had not earned this contract and it was awful to see the majority of the city council vote for this action. Standing upon the dais, I made my opinion known by saying that I was rushing home after the meeting to shower off the filth that was covering this decision. The blatant favoritism made me sick. Balance was restored when the city was sued and—after many years of litigation—the original company was given the contract back.

I remember a line from the poem "*A Gloria*" that has stayed with me since I encountered it in my Spanish class in Mexico. A translation of the line would read: "There are birds that fly through swamps and emerge clean; my feathers are made of the same kind." In politics I flew through many muddy swamps and saw filth all around me. Staying true to my life's purpose and mission gave me the strength to keep flying through and emerge with my integrity intact. Make sure that you do not give someone the power to ruffle or dirty your feathers.

There will be times when someone will take credit for work that still glistens from your fresh sweat. In the worst cases, your work will not even be acknowledged, your name will not even be mentioned, and you'll feel like a ghost filled with resentment. This can be infuriating and certainly hard to stomach. I specifically recall one of my colleagues who seemed to pop up out of nowhere for photo opportunities. It was difficult to watch her smile for the cameras when I knew that I had been the one who worked tirelessly on the project. She could claim victory and seem proud, but she could never enjoy the glory of knowing, like I did, that it was my hard work that got us there. There was some consolation in knowing that those surrounding me also knew that it was my hard work that was being acknowledged with a photograph or newspaper story.

Even today, I often open up the newspaper to read how politicians are being charged with conflict of interest, corruption, extortion, and the list goes on. I wonder how people who almost certainly began their work in government with the noblest intentions and a clear commitment end up behind bars. It not only boggles my mind, but it offends and, more than anything else, saddens me because it gives politics a bad name.

Regrettably, I've seen many people in both business and politics who worked hard to get to a position of power only to be consumed by it. Power can be overwhelming when you've never had it and don't know how to manage it. And other times, it can be like a drug.

Power As an Addiction

It's tragic when I see people fight tooth and nail to keep whatever power they hold. Unfortunately, these people have allowed power to define their existence. They place the greatest emphasis on what's least important: their titles, office locations, office furniture, number of assistants around them, number of advisors they have, and so forth. They have completely internalized what others have said of them, especially the praise. They read the press releases coming out of their offices that describe their accomplishments and think only of how they could add more achievements to their lists. Unknowingly, such people have defeated the whole purpose of power to do good in the world by becoming slaves to it.

Evidence of this was all around me when I saw how desperate people became when they knew that their time in office was coming to a close. They could not comprehend how life would go on after their appointments or elected offices were over. Rather than seeing the opportunities lying all around them, they'd let their ethics dissipate as they fought to hold on to what they believed was power. They were no longer guided by a sense of purpose or service, but only by what had grown to be an insatiable thirst. The lengths to which people will go is alarming. Like slaves and prisoners, they often end up behind actual bars.

I have always tried to remain humble in the presence of any power that has been given to me. I have reminded myself that whatever perceived power I had was given to me by others with one hand and could easily be taken away with the other. Nothing was more humbling than knowing that my community had elected me to a position of influence, trusting that I would look after their best interests. It was truly an enlightening moment when I first took the oath of elected office. As I was repeating the oath, I took it to heart. It was at the moment when it struck me with a startling clarity that people were entrusting me with their well-being. They chose me over other people to make choices for them.

Although I've taken the oath of office several times—as an appointed or elected official—it has not lost its effect on me. When my presidential commission document came to my office at the Treasury, I read it over and over again. Eventually, I placed it on the wall near my desk to serve as a guiding light and reminder before taking my seat each morning. The series of words described the qualities that had helped me attain my position and the expectations of my behavior that came with being treasurer. I can recite it from memory: "Know ye that reposing especial trust and confidence in the integrity, diligence, and discretion of Rosario Marín of California, I have nominated and by and with the advice and consent of the Senate do appoint her the Treasurer of the United States." I was conscious of the fact that this was the highest distinction I had held up until this point in my life. I felt humbled by a position that had only been offered to forty people before me. I was—and still am—grateful for that honor. Why would I, in this position of power, do anything to even raise a question as to my integrity? The president expected the highest degree of conduct from me and that is exactly what I delivered.

Today when I speak with new council members or people who want to go into public service, I always tell them that the most critical question they could ask themselves before making any decision is whether they are acting in the best interests of the people they represent. It's that simple. If the answer is ever no, then they cannot move forward with a clear conscience. You'd think that this would be common sense, but I have come across countless examples where I am sure politicians and others didn't take the few minutes necessary to ask themselves the important questions. It's as though people forget why they were elected or appointed. It will be difficult for you to go wrong if you proceed with what you believe is best for the people who will be affected by your decision.

The Wise Use of Power

When I worked in the office of community relations for Governor Wilson, I was aware of how a call from my department could disrupt the regular workday of other departments and councils. They would feel like they had to drop whatever it was that they were working on in order to get what anyone from our office needed. I had experienced this firsthand while working in various departments and councils prior to my position with the governor. We were trained to make sure that at the drop of a hat we responded to anything the governor's office requested. The first step was always to let our supervisors know and they, in turn, ensured that our response was as rapid as possible.

Being cognizant of how disruptive a call from me could be, I went to great lengths to make sure people would not fall all over themselves just because we were calling. I clearly explained what I needed and asked that it be done within a specific and reasonable time frame. I was respectful of their everyday jobs and made sure that they knew I was aware of their limited resources. The person on the other end of the line always seemed appreciative of my delivery. As a result, I knew that I could call on them whenever I truly needed them.

The governor had taught us how to distinguish among levels of importance and urgency. In prioritizing my work-load, I'd deal with the most important items first to ensure that any sense of urgency was greatly reduced. The governor disliked the frenzied environment that resulted from some-one's not giving a task the appropriate importance at the appropriate time. He believed that last-minute emergencies should rarely occur. I couldn't have agreed more and made sure not to contribute to anyone's already hectic day due to last-minute requests.

I learned that judiciously using whatever power working for the office of the governor gave me resulted in a mutual respect among everyone I came across. I understood that power is of no use if it is wielded without purpose. Direct, clear, and purposeful action is the best way to go.

Please Use Your Power

As our travels together wind down, I hope that if you have gained anything from reading my life's story, it is that power can and should be used for good. Nothing is more frustrating than observing people who have achieved a powerful position only to abuse or squander it. It has taken so much work, time, energy, and effort to arrive, and when they do, they ruin it. This is especially painful to see when it occurs with minorities and women who have attained positions of influence. Having overcome more barriers than others, some get embroiled in scandals and fail to accomplish anything. Why would they waver and give up the convictions that got them to where they stand?

As I've perhaps already made clear, I almost always gravitate toward becoming an advocate for the underdog of the underdogs. When I was an advocate for people with disabilities, I'd advocate even more for the racial minorities within that group. When a member of Hispanic groups, I advocated for Hispanics with disabilities. As mayor of an already poor and disenfranchised city, I attempted to help the most poor. As treasurer, I attempted to help the unbanked population through financial literacy efforts.

Politics often get personal for me given my background. No matter what, I'll always ferociously defend the poor, abused, and the disabled. I feel no need to make excuses or apologies. Anybody who knows me knows where I stand on the issues. Those who don't know me learn my views rather quickly because I wear them on my sleeve.

When I was the mayor of my city, it was incredibly important for me to enable business owners to succeed through improving the business climate of the city. Although I am as strong an enforcer of the law as they come, I've also been involved in the development of regulations; I know how they can be interpreted in the field, and sometimes, discretionary leeway is allowed. I understand the need to grant exceptions if it is for the greater good and within your power to do so.

My community development director would hear from me every now and then when I believed we were imposing severe barriers, especially on small businesses. At times, our regulations were so burdensome that I would tell him that we were driving them into bankruptcy before they even had a chance to open for business. Business owners would talk to me about their struggles and complain about all of our regulations that needed to be met by the deadlines our office set.

One specific business owner thought he had taken care of every last detail. He had spent a small fortune on radio, television, and newspaper advertising leading up to his grand opening. His entrepreneurial spirit was admirable. During the final inspection, however, it was noticed that planters—meant to act as barriers—were not as large as we had requested. It was decided that he would have to postpone his much-anticipated grand opening. To add to his distress, city hall is closed on Fridays, and there was no time to set up another inspection even if he had been able to fix the problem in accordance with our regulations. Of course, it was not the inspectors' job (or within their power) to take into consideration the great amount of money that the business owner had poured into the opening of the store.

The owner got hold of me and explained his situation. My heart went out to him, and although I could have easily told him that he would have to wait like everybody else until city hall was open, what would anyone gain from that? I told him that I'd do anything in my power to make sure that his grand opening would come to fruition. I quickly set up a meeting between the city's engineer and the code enforcement people. With a little bit of help, this small business owner was able to open as scheduled and everyone was happy. Code enforcement did their job, the city engineer assessed the safety of the barriers, and I was able to use my position to help a small-business owner whose business has produced significant tax revenue for the city ever since. I made a decision that exceptions needed to be granted in this case because no amount of planning could have prepared the business owner for this last-minute regulation. I decided that it wasn't in the best interest of the city or those we serve to not have this business open on time.

Another example of using power for good was when I brought attention to the horrible state of our schools. I fought for our schools to secede from the Los Angeles Unified School District. Being part of that school district was doing nothing to help with the astronomical and unacceptable 60 percent dropout rate. That kind of statistic doesn't just happen overnight. Although its causes are varied, it certainly doesn't help that our residents had not been paid attention to in a long time. It seemed as though the problems that occurred in Huntington Park and in other southeast cities barely registered on the political radar.

The dropout rate is still a long way from being acceptable, but great strides were made when the independent cities in the southeast area of Los Angeles joined forces to finally get several of the long-standing issues some attention. We became very vocal and made such noise that eventually the district started building more schools in our area. I was, fortunately, able to use my power to highlight this very difficult problem. I knew that it was my duty. It would have been of no use if I simply sat back and played with my power as though it were some sort of toy. It was certainly put to much better use as a tool for change.

Earning the Right to Wear Pink

Before I bid you a final adieu, I have to ask: What will a powerful person like you wear for the journey ahead? What colors will best represent the power that lies within you to the outside world? Isn't it a truly satisfying feeling to reach a stage in your life where you are confident enough to wear whatever colors you'd like?

We may not have had a lot of money growing up, but my family took a lot of pride in how we presented ourselves. I know that, whether consciously or subconsciously, people do judge a book by its cover. I pondered this quite a bit when I was about to be featured in *Hispanic Business* magazine, and everyone had an opinion as to what color I should wear.

I had always been aware of the colors I wore when transacting business or while working in politics. When I was hired for my first job, I read a wonderful book titled *Dress for Success* and followed its guidelines to a T. On my climb up the ladder, I made sure that—even if it set me back a few dollars—I was outfitted "properly" in colors that were "appropriate" to my working environment. At the bank, that meant black, pinstripe blue, navy blue, and gray. I had so many black suits that I'd have been prepared to attend a midday funeral at the drop of a hat. As I rose professionally, common wisdom said that red was the way to go if I wanted to subtly send power messages.

So, it didn't come as a surprise that when trying to make a decision for the magazine cover, many on my staff suggested red to make it loud and clear that I was the highest-ranking Latina in the president's administration. A few others on staff suggested that I should wear navy blue, the color of business. Somebody else thought I should wear green because it is the color of money. Then came the suggestion of royal blue because I had made history as the first immigrant to reach the position of treasurer.

After carefully listening to the suggestions, I simply said thank you.

"So, what color are you going to wear?" everyone asked in unison.

"Pink!" I said proudly.

I laughed as I saw the perplexed looks surround me. I decided that if people were going to judge this book by its cover, it would be clad in a pink suit. People thought I was crazy to even consider wearing such a color for the cover of a business magazine. I explained to them how I hoped the title of treasurer of the United States spoke for itself. I no longer felt a need to broadcast a sense of power by wearing red or any other color. I had earned the right to wear whatever color I wanted. I like pink, so pink it was.

I heard a lot of comments once the magazine hit newsstands. Many people, especially women, said that seeing me in pink emboldened them to wear the colors they felt most comfortable in. A woman I met a few months later told me that she purchased the magazine to find out more about the *atrevida,* or brazen woman, who dared to wear pink on the cover of a business magazine. She ended our exchange with: "You go, girl!"

Today, flipping through my closet, I realize I own practically every color I might want to wear—evidence of a long and rewarding journey. I don't pay too much attention to which colors are appropriate for each season; I just pick what I feel like wearing. The message I hope to send is simple: I have arrived and I can wear whatever color my heart desires.

Sadly, our time together has come to a close. Whatever your own mission is in life, I pray that you experience the sacred joy of knowing that what you do matters to someone, that as a result of your efforts today, your family and community are better off than yesterday, and you can be grateful for doing God's work here on earth. Good luck and safe travels on your own journey. I'll be with you in spirit.

Acknowledgments

The creation of a book is a fascinating process. I have had the luxury of having many people's encouragement and support all throughout this process. But I would be remiss if I did not acknowledge Johanna Castillo's conviction in the power of my story; Christine Rubin's time and effort in reading the draft and crystallizing some ideas; my dear friend Shirley Wheat whose research was absolutely necessary; and Sean Walsh and Dan Zingale for reading the manuscripts and ensuring the last details were complete. Last but not least, I want to thank Carlos Queirós, whose guidance was invaluable to the development of this book.